This book is fo

If you are a busy city business exec
lives a stressed, exhausted and ove........
for you. If you want to transform your mindset, have boundless amounts of energy and have real physical presence through improved movement patterns and posture, then this book can help you become more productive, energetic and accelerate your career.

This book is for you if you want to achieve

- Work/life balance

- A good night's sleep

- A positive attitude

- Your goals through behaviour change

- Real physical presence

- Energy in abundance and

- A competitive advantage in the workplace

What people are saying about Adam

"Adam's approach to mastering your own destiny resonates with my own experience - the work is spot on when it comes to a perfect work, life and health balance."

Sean Wall Executive Vice-President
Network Operations and Aviation for DHL

"A practical guide to get fit with fantastic tips... highly recommend this book!"

Darshana Ubl CEO of Entrevo

"This book is full of straightforward yet empowering tools to motivate you to make small changes to achieve a healthy balanced life in all your spheres of influence. There's nothing to lose and everything to gain by this journey"

Arpita Dutt   Partner at Brahams, Dutt, Badrick and French
UK Top 100 Employment lawyers

"I've trained with Adam for a number of years. His expertise and encouragement have been invaluable not just in helping me improve and maintain my physical health but also in helping guide me with my nutrition and stress-management. Adam is also great fun to work with so that even when the going gets tough and I'm being pushed to the next level, there's always time for a joke and plenty of laughter - vital components of well-being and feeling good!"

David G (Suffolk)

"Adam puts the fun back into training. His sessions give variety and a full body workout, without just focusing on the main muscles. His vast and varied knowledge of nutrition and the dynamics of how the human body works helps him tailor the right sessions so you can meet your goals in the right way."

Prakash Radhakrishnan (Berkshire, UK)

"My posture is poor and I suffer with painful hips and back because of how I stand. I have been training with Adam through his personal training sessions for about 12 months; my posture has improved – as well as my stamina and general fitness.

"His sports science degree, training and background in athletics all contribute to the fact that he really does understand the body, and he uses different techniques and varies the exercises we do each time – testing and changing until we find the one that works.

"I would not hesitate to recommend him. His knowledge and experience means that you get a totally different type of personal training than you would at a gym. This is tailored to you, and Adam spends the first session assessing your needs before starting a programme that is just for you."

Louise Walker (Buckinghamshire, UK)

"I have been working with Adam as my personal trainer for fitness or nutrition over the last 5 years. The main reason for my continued work with Adam, is due to the enthusiasm he has for the helping me to achieve my goals. If you are committed to achieving them, Adam will help you get there; he expects nothing less than 100% commitment from you when taking part in any of his programmes. I have found Adam's knowledge of fitness, nutrition and the human body and mind to be second to none. He will tailor individual sessions to your needs and you certainly feel like you have benefited from each session."

Ricky Raithaitha (Berkshire, UK)

"Adam is an exceptional heath and wellness expert. Having known Adam for a little over 5 months now, his expertise and his ability to challenge 'Why' I am doing what I am doing has made a huge difference to my health, wealth and happiness. A healthy body and mind has enabled me to work smarter and be more productive, plus I can now lift things again as he has sorted out my shoulder pain. He is not a PT trainer, but someone who knows more about fitness and

health for well-being, and is a must see if you are wanting to get more out of your workday and personal life. Highly recommend you take out one of Adams programmes."

Amanda Kennedy (Surrey, UK)

"Adam Strong has been my personal trainer for a couple of years. The results I have achieved to date are largely due to Adam's perfect combination of various training methods, individualised exercise programmes and challenging yet achievable goal setting. Adam's professionalism, extensive knowledge and enthusiastic commitment to his work and ultimately his clients, offers the perfect scenario for success and he can set the foundations for a new healthier lifestyle!

"Adam is passionate about fitness and it shows through the energy and enthusiasm that he brings to each session. His easy-going, friendly personality creates a relaxed, comfortable atmosphere. Adam makes each workout challenging and most importantly fun. He also places a high value on precise form with each exercise. He encourages me to push past my perceived limits to get results. I have energy; my balance and flexibility have improved enormously. If you are serious about changing your life for the better, Adam will lead you every step of the way."

Richard Rouse (Berkshire, UK)

About the Author

Adam Strong is a highly successful fitness guru, athlete, movement specialist and trainer. Adam is a true ambassador for the fitness industry. He teaches and writes courses from basic NVQ level through to those covering chain reaction biomechanics.

He is the creator of a revolutionary 12-step programme designed for executives and companies who want to achieve peak performance. He uses techniques in sports performance, mindset and nutrition to enhance physical and mental well-being. His clients know him for his skills in addressing work / life balance, stress issues, and movement and function. Adam's clients can expect to be more productive and achieve greater things in their career and personal life.

Adam lives in Windsor, Berkshire. His passions include travel, scuba diving, sport, and anything to do with the sea, plus - most important of all - spending time with his children.

Acknowledgements

I would like to thank a huge amount of people in their support of helping me become a Key Person of Influence in my industry.

Firstly to my wonderful client and friend, David Gibbons, who has helped and supported me over the years as well as helping me form this into a well-structured book.

Secondly to a wonderful lady that has been my rock throughout my journey, Amanda Kennedy. She is an expert in marketing and PR that has helped me raise my profile in my industry.

I also want to thank another awesome client and friend, Louise Walker. I don't think she really understands how much she means to me. She has helped me in so many ways that made me think about my business seriously and introduced me to the Key Person of Influence business course in which I have learnt so much from.

I want to thank all of the experts including Daniel Priestley, Andrew Priestley, Darshana Ubl, Mike Harris, Mindy-Gibbons Klein, Nic Rixon, Penny Power and Julia Langkraehr for supporting me on my journey.

A big thank you to Chris Day from Filament Publishing for supporting and believing in me, my illustrator Katherine Burgess and Ricky Raithathia, client and friend.

And on top of that, my clients, friends and family that have believed and supported me over the years.

Dedication

This book is dedicated to my two children,

Leo and Paige,

who I love with all my heart and cherish

every moment with.

Daddy is so proud of whom you have become today.

A gift for you!

As a companion to this book, I have created a special report **"5 Top Tips to maximise fat loss, energy levels and motivation"** to help you to become more motivated, productive and energetic.

It is full of lots of gems to help you to achieve peak performance in the business world by developing a competitive mindset, look and feeling the best at what you do.

Download it free from my website
www.xclusivecorporatefitness.com

Move it or Lose it!

**A step by step approach
to achieving peak performance
in the corporate world
through mindset, fitness
and nutrition**

Adam Strong Bsc (Hons)

Published by
Filament Publishing Ltd
16, Croydon Road, Waddon, Croydon,
Surrey, CR0 4PA, United Kingdom
Telephone +44 (0)20 8688 2598
Fax +44 (0)20 7183 7186
info@filamentpublishing.com
www.filamentpublishing.com

ISBN 978-1-908691-87-3

Printed by Berforts Information Press

Contents

Introduction

You're probably thinking why a personal trainer, such as me, is writing a book to help you 'embrace and live your life'. Well, first of all I'm no ordinary personal trainer; I'm regarded in my industry as an athlete, coach, mentor, problem solver and teacher. Apart from my qualifications and experience in the fitness industry, I'm writing this book from the perspective of giving everyone who leads a pressurised working life the means to effect a positive lifestyle transformation by creating a sensible work/life balance and improving their fitness and well-being. I want to offer you the advice and support that I've been privileged to give to my personal clients over the years. This includes some great tools for change, and proven techniques to help you de-stress and re-energise yourself.

Clearly, this book is not designed to take the place of a healthcare practitioner. My aim is simply to help you make a unique change in your life, transforming how you think about yourself and others. I offer a holistic approach to lifestyle changes, focused on real solutions to real problems. And reflecting this practical approach, there are a variety of tasks and challenges throughout the book that I encourage you to complete to help you get the most out of your reading.

Where I'm coming from....

I am eternally grateful for those people in my life that have helped me reach the top of my game. I'm in great shape both mentally and physically plus I have more personal freedom to choose what I do, how I do it and when I want to do it. But it certainly hasn't always been easy and I've had to overcome a number of obstacles in my life.

Growing up was tough. My parents separated shortly after I was born and we struggled financially. I developed alopecia at the age of eight and was regularly bullied at school. This had a massive impact on my self-confidence, self-esteem and relationships. Nevertheless, a bright spot was that right from my earliest years, I've always been a keen sportsman. I started long-distance running at the age of 11, progressing to become one of the youngest and most promising athletes in Surrey. At the age of 13, I decided to join my local athletics club where I trained with Mo Farah who became a good training partner. Long-distance running and athletics offered me the opportunity to escape from my family problems and allowed me to succeed at something and feel good about myself. Unfortunately, in my teens, life issues started to interfere as I lost my focus. My mindset changed and I no longer believed in myself. I wanted to be the best but I simply didn't have the willpower, encouragement or support from others around me to enable me to stay focused and maintain and develop my sporting potential.

I became someone who just followed the herd. I left school at 16, beginning work at McDonald's where, against the odds, I knuckled down and progressed to Assistant Manager. But after a number of years, I felt I was becoming part of the McDonald's 'wallpaper' and might end up working there forever! I realised that my dream was not to work in fast food for the rest of my life but to pursue my dream career.

I realised that there was only person who was stopping me from doing something with my life and being a success. Me!! By sorting out what I really wanted from life, I began to turn my life around. I found my way back into cross-country running and through a combination of self-belief and self-discipline, enabled myself to get my dream job on a cruise ship - a far cry from my previous existence. Since then, I've completely transformed my life, progressing to become a recognised leader in the health and fitness industry.

Now, as I continue to grow my career, it's my purpose to help inspire and empower others to succeed and achieve their dreams.

But for many people in today's pressurised, highly competitive business world, the dream that we can live our lives on our own terms is fading away. Tough economic conditions and 24/7 business culture mean that however successful we become, we have to work harder still, putting in longer hours and taking on more responsibilities. All this comes at a cost!!

It's a fact that people living highly pressurised working lives are likely to die ten years earlier than those in less demanding roles. There is a strong correlation between lifestyle diseases and exhausted and burnt-out employees (Van Gaal, L. et al 2006, Ceriello and Motz 2004).

Many people simply take their health for granted and push their body to the limits. I've known individuals have heart attacks at the age of 54. Three out of four clients who come to me suffer from high blood pressure and many are either border-line type 2 diabetic or already have it.

To be diagnosed with a serious condition that you'll have to live with for the rest of your entire life is not just frightening and shocking - it's a game-changer. While declining health will eventually affect us all, we do have the power and the choice to make sure we stay healthy and fit for as long as possible. Now is the time to do something about it before it's too late!

You weren't born to work; you were born to live!

This book is a wake-up call. Health is your No. 1 priority - that's a fact!!

In these pages, you'll discover that there is light at the end of the tunnel and that you can achieve the 'sweet spot' in your life. I aim to give you the means to re-energise your mind and body. So 'step-up' and act before it's too late!

Be aware that this book is designed to challenge you. It sets out a number of questions you need to ask yourself and the key activities you need to follow through on. To get maximum benefit, ideally you shouldn't move on until you've completed each question or activity in turn, but if you're unable to do this, do make sure you go back afterwards to complete them. The questions and activities are designed to challenge you and get you thinking by pushing your 'hot buttons' to create the solutions for a healthy lifestyle. The book sets out a pathway for establishing a work/life balance that hopefully will meet your needs, no matter what challenges or obstacles you face. The aim is to get you living your life as you want it to be.

You might want to read it again!!

This book is not a magic pill, nor is it a quick-fix solution. It requires you to make an investment in your health and well-being. My approach is holistic, incorporating steps for creating a healthy lifestyle, dealing with excess stress and making your life that little bit easier. The book will help you assess your own health and fitness needs, identifying problems and providing you with the solutions to fix them.

Your day-to-day health is very much a reflection of the way you live your life. I'll give you tips on how to get a good night's sleep, put stress management techniques into practice and how to deal with negative thinking. We'll also cover your ego, motivation and self-esteem. I'm going to challenge you to start your lifestyle transformation today. The book will help you formulate a plan - a workable approach that many executives don't normally have access to.

But to get the most out of the programme, it's vital that you engage fully and act on the recommendations and tasks. Throughout the book, you'll also see that I do recognise that making such lifestyle changes isn't always easy - so I do aim to make the programme workable and build in some 'give and take' - just like being in a relationship!

Finally, you will be given the opportunity to 'step up' and make an action plan. This will include introducing high-quality nutritious foods into your diet and building a realistic exercise programme. We'll aim to change the way you think about your life, creating a more youthful, vibrant you in the process. After all, you're only as old as you think you are!

Most importantly, all readers of this book should realise that fitness and well-being aren't just for 'other people'. They are achievable by anyone. But you do need focus, belief and discipline.

I'm confident that reading this book will give you the opportunity and means to change your life and live the type of life you want. Not only this, I believe the changes you make will positively impact the lives of those around you.

Good luck and I hope you love reading my book!

Adam

*Take care of
your body.
It's the only
place you have
to live.*

Jim Rohn

Chapter 1: Burning out

My years of experience in the fitness and well-being industry have shown me that clients come to me because they are ready to make a change and in a position to do so. So it's important to understand where you are in your life at the present time. Although a successful leader, you may be beginning to understand your limitations, e.g. that you're not a superhero and that you don't have endless amounts of energy. You may be realising the importance of setting boundaries in your life.

Most business people find their working lives stressful at the best of times. And often as we progress in our careers, we have to cope with higher and higher stress levels day in, day out. Have you ever had the feeling that the pressure is too much and that something needs to give?

Stress in the workplace is commonly caused by excessive demands, impossible deadlines and long working hours (Chapman, L. 2012). Executives have to have the tools to deal with the high pressures of corporate life in an increasingly competitive environment. Just as important, they need to maintain their earnings potential and continue to be recognised as the best person to do the job. My question is what would happen if you felt like you couldn't meet those demands or live up to those standards, or if you felt your boss wasn't giving you the credit that you deserve? Have you run out of ideas about how to be the best and ensure your success? Well, I hope not!

The fact is that the most successful business leaders use lifestyle management methods to enable them to become even more productive, energetic and focused. Based on this approach, I work to help my clients explore some of the reasons why they think they're not as successful as they could be, how to unlock their full potential as a successful business leader, and to identify those techniques that have or have not worked for them in the past.

Have you ever been in a position where you simply have nothing left in the gas tank? Are you running on empty or feel you need to recharge your batteries? Burnout is a condition of emotional, physical and mental exhaustion, caused mainly by prolonged and relenting periods of stress. Becoming burnt out significantly reduces your capacity to function, affecting both your productivity and your ability to deal with new challenges. You may start to feel useless and even resentful towards your colleagues, family and friends. But still you have to keep going - focusing on your end-of-year bonus, ensuring your bosses think you're doing a good job and, of course, keeping everyone else happy. It may be that things have reached such a level that you really don't care about life right now. You may feel ignored or simply beyond caring.

Story: A few years ago, I met a young stockbroker who had been in the industry for about four years. I asked him what life was like being a stockbroker. I thought his response was going to be that he loved earning lots of cash and enjoyed his life with his flash cars and a big house, but I was quite surprised by his response. He told me that life on the trading floor was extremely stressful; he told me that he and his fellow stockbroker peers had to find ways to adapt to the daily stress of making big financial decisions that involved winning and losing huge sums of money for their clients. He felt great making money but felt terrible about losing money that wasn't his. In fact, he said the more experienced stockbrokers became, the less financially motivated they became towards earning lots of money. In just a short number of years, many stockbrokers experienced 'burnout' and left.

You may feel as if you're just a cog in a wheel or 'going through the motions' each day.

<u>Your routine may look like this:</u> get up at 5am after an awful night's sleep, reach for multiple caffeine fixes without any breakfast, catch up with emails, grab your briefcase and out the door at 6.30am. Catch the overcrowded train at 7am, have a sandwich at lunchtime whilst still on the computer, finish work at 6-7pm. You get home around 8pm, eat a large ready meal, catch up on emails again and then get to bed by midnight. Is this you? If this is, you need to wake up because if you're not totally burnt out now, it will be only a matter of time. You may feel paranoid and withdrawn at times, which can often lead to isolation and no sense of control. Do you feel overworked and undervalued in your organisation?

It's not uncommon for business executives to work 60, 70 or 80 hours a week understandably, as their commitment and sense of responsibility can make it difficult to say 'No'. Your lifestyle can seriously be affected and there can be a significant impact on your sleep patterns resulting in lack of sleep. We will be looking at this further in the book. You may also feel a lack of close and supportive relationships. Self-doubt may start to creep in leading to a lack of motivation. Do you suffer from regular headaches, joint pain or colds and flu? This could be because stress is affecting and suppressing your immune system.

 Activity: How do you view your life and in what direction is it heading right now? Write down your thoughts.

Reigniting the fire!!

There are a number of strategies that may help in a burnout situation but they're not going to be suited to everyone's needs. Firstly, let's look at the mind and your cognitive thought process. Most executives will use the left side of their brain (the logical side), which can tend to get overworked. However, it is the right side of the brain (the creative side) that we must learn to nourish and build our success on. You should consider taking a break from technology. This includes your laptop, tablet, cell phone, emails, financial reports or anything that is related to work/business, which stays at work.

As an executive you need to be adaptable, which means getting access to and using resources around you. These additional resources are all around you and can be easily accessible as you're the boss and have most of the control! Use your personal assistant to organise meetings with a client or delegate tasks so it can free up time for you so that you can do the things that you want to do. If you're not in that position or you feel that you can't move forward, then go to your superior and explain the situation. I would certainly ask for clarification of your job description, as most executives end up taking on many additional responsibilities. Consider asking for new tasks and challenges that could revitalise your working career. If you feel that really is not an option, then you clearly need a better solution; take time off to recharge those batteries or simply change your job altogether!

We don't live in a perfect world with perfect people around us. If we did, it simply would be a very unstimulating world! Stress is good for us but not overwhelmingly so. All executives get stressed - that's a way of life - but all of us react in different ways so therefore one approach is not going to suit everyone. We are all subjected to stress in any shape or form. For example, there is never enough time in the day with competing work commitments, family responsibilities, and sales targets to meet. In reality, all these stresses in your life can be controlled. Stress should be manageable, allowing you to be in control of your thoughts, emotions and schedule, and how you deal with problems subconsciously.

Would you like to know how to cope with stress more effectively?

To manage stress effectively, we must first identify the source!! Sometimes this isn't as obvious as you may think but commonly it could be work deadlines or work demands or sometimes just procrastination. The key is knowing how to overcome those hurdles.

The source of stress is heavily linked to your habits, attitudes and excuses. What are you stressed about right now and do you have control over the cause?

You may find that being in a high-pressured environment, it is tempting to opt for easy - and unhealthy - ways to cope. These may include smoking, drinking too much alcohol, overeating or, in some cases, under eating, using medication such as anti-depressants or muscle relaxants, drugs, sleeping too much, withdrawing from friends, family and hobbies, or taking out your anxiety on other people, e.g. through angry outbursts or even physical violence.

Stress can have both physiological and psychological side effects that can lead to digestive issues, such as irritable bowel syndrome (IBS) and constipation and anxiety.

Is this the way you deal with stress? There are much healthier ways to cope but in order to deal with stress more effectively you must either change your situation or change the way you react.

My first strategy for you is to avoid the unnecessary and to teach yourself how to say **'No'**! That means not taking too much on so that you can't handle it. Don't feel as if you need to say 'Yes' to work all the time. You may feel you still need to make that all-important impression but your organisation will still survive and this could be a good opportunity to delegate some of your tasks to someone else.

There are a number of ways to deal with negativity. Firstly, if you have to work with negative people then help them to become more positive. Use some of your skills and experience to help overcome their negativity. Or consider staying away from these negative people. You will be amazed how negative people can drain you physically, mentally and emotionally. Remember also that your other colleagues can equally be affected and sucked into the reach of the negative-thinkers. You must blank them out and ignore them.

One of the biggest things that can really stress me out and put me in a negative mindset is watching or reading the news. I used to watch the news regularly and read the newspaper on the train like everyone else. But the only news that everyone ever talks about is negative!! Someone has been murdered, the economy is shrinking, and people are losing their jobs. Don't you find it's actually just a distraction? The more the media influences you, the more that you will begin to believe that there is no money or jobs and everything is failing. It serves no purpose; it doesn't help you in your job and, in most cases, isn't relevant to your life. The media thrives on negativity. But most news is out of our control and, in most circumstances, it only affects us indirectly or does not affect us at all. If there is going to be a nuclear war then trust me, the news will reach you one way or another so you're not going to miss out! If you take a break from the news, I guarantee your mindset will change positively.

 Write down what stresses you out and prioritise with the 'musts' at the top (need to be dealt with ASAP) and the 'shoulds' (less important) towards the bottom…

Commuting can often stress people out (stressor) so the solution could be change your routes home, leave earlier or later.

	Stressor	What I need to do to change the situation?
1.		
2.		
3.		
4.		
5.		
6.		
7.		
8.		
9.		
10.		

From time to time, stress is unavoidable. However it can be managed by altering the situation. You can change things so the problem doesn't keep reappearing. I always find that the best way to change things is to get things off my chest rather than bottling them up. Speak to someone you trust about it. This might be a colleague, a superior, or your HR director. By bottling things up, your tension and anxiety will continue to build, but by talking about them, you'll start to eradicate them.

Stress can be managed but first you must take control and look at particular situations from a more positive perspective and learn to adapt as well. If you're travelling on a train to your next meeting and it's running late, there is nothing you can do. It's simply out of your control. Instead, try taking the approach of turning the situation into an opportunity by pausing and reflecting on your own life. I always find that self-evaluation is an excellent way to make improvements in my life.

On the next page, make a list of all your achievements and accomplishments, however big or small and on both a personal and business level, then write down how you felt at the time. Look back on your past. It could be something that is deep in your memory banks which has made a big difference to the person you are today. For example, I still remember being in the Cubs as a youngster and my motivation to work for as many badges as possible to show them on my uniform. I loved the recognition my badges gave me. It made me a bigger and better person. By doing this, you will really begin to appreciate your life and regain your sense of purpose in living.

1.

2.

3.

4.

5.

6.

7.

8.

9.

10.

Story: I have a very good friend of mine who also works in the fitness industry. I love talking about him and his life. He lives his life in the fast lane and recently he took on a new senior job position. He also started in a new personal relationship and began on a high intensity entrepreneur business course. He also had his current client base to service as well.

However, in a short space of time, the realisation kicked in that these new things he was taking on were more challenging then he thought. His work was affected; his relationship with his new girlfriend was already on the rocks and he found he could not deliver the kind of service that his clients expected of him. He had taken on too much. He never stopped and he simply could not switch off. In that short space of time, his stress and anxiety levels hit new highs. He was virtually burnt out!

I advised him he needed some time away so that he could gather his thoughts and prioritise his life. So he booked a last minute holiday to get himself together. He told me that it gave him time to reflect and assess what was important in his life. It gave him the time to switch off and find the answers to overcoming his challenges. It also gave him time for relaxation and for his body and mind to recuperate.

"Challenges are what make life interesting and overcoming them makes life meaningful."

Joshua J. Marine

Another view I have about stress is that the only time it ever rains, it then pours! Do you ever get that feeling? Everything happens at the same time. And it's normally the type of stressful situation that is completely out of your hands. So don't try to control the uncontrollable. Just focus on the things that you can control. If you face a particular major challenge, then look on it as an opportunity to grow and become stronger. If you've made a poor decision that has contributed to your stressful situation, then reflect and think how you could learn from this and what you can do to change it for the better next time.

If in your business role you sometimes feel rather isolated or if you are travelling a lot, call up a colleague or a trusted friend and express your feelings as somebody else's input may help you resolve the situation or at least to share the problem.

In the business world where tensions are high and competition is fierce, I have known executives come under so much stress that their body switches to the flight/fight response. This is a short-term response where the body simply cannot sustain long periods of high-energy demands that is being placed on it. In this situation, people just switch off and literally live off adrenalin to try and keep going. This adrenalin will literally help them work harder, compete more fiercely and push anyone aside that gets in their pathway.

These types of executives are out to survive and see everyone around them as a threat to their achievements, job, position in the company and bonuses. Executives will experience this response if they get frustrated and challenged in certain situations. If you have ever experienced the fight/flight response, it will always result in negative consequences. You will feel like you have the power but no sense of control. You become excitable, anxious, jumpy and irritable. This reduces your ability to effectively work with those around you.

Things that relax me.....

Your heart rate increases and beats like a drum. You sweat profusely and it is often difficult to stay focused and in control. The intense need to survive interferes with your ability to make good decisions so you tend to make more mistakes and accidents are more common.

Hiding under a rock is not going to do you any good from my past experience. I used to find it hard to simply switch off; my subconscious mind would just keep firing off like a firework display, one business idea after the other!

Managing stress can often feel unmanageable but here are some great healthy ways to make your life more manageable. One of the key things I do is to set aside some relaxation time. This means making uninterrupted time for myself away from the hustle and bustle without having to think about my responsibilities. Also a great way to relax and de-stress is to find some time for laughter, e.g. at a local comedy club, watching a comedian on TV or just getting together with friends. Laughter always provides the opportunity to put a smile on everyone's face. Another way to manage stress could be on a more spiritual level. This might include meditation or listening to calming music. Yoga and pilates are great ways too. Another method that really helped me personally is developing a routine of walking along the River Thames near to where I live. I often just sit on the boat jetty - absolute peace and tranquillity! I find this is a great way to help me relax, as I love being near water.

Following your different hobbies is also a great way of relaxing. Everyone is different and all of us can find various ways of successfully relaxing.

 Make a list of things that relax you and put them into your schedule.........

When the negative
thoughts come -
and they will;
they come to all of us -
it's not enough to just
not dwell on it...
You've got to replace
it with a positive
thought.

Joel Osteen

Dealing with negative thinking

What's the talk of the town these days? Well it must be the economy!! People losing their jobs, the Eurozone in crisis, businesses going bust, the pound against the dollar.... the list is endless! With such media focus, no wonder people are ever more concerned about job security these days. The media is one of the biggest sources of encouraging negative thinking. It drives me bonkers! Negative thinking is similar to uncontrollable stress in the impact it can have on our lives. We cannot control the media - we simply don't have the resources. Tune out from the media. That's the best way that you can stay focused and succeed.

As an executive you will probably find that some of your work peers can also be quite negative people and that this tends to change the mood and atmosphere in a work environment. I call these negative people 'Mood Hoovers'. These types of people literally 'suck up' the positive thoughts and aspirations of others - just like a vacuum cleaner! If you've ever heard of the saying, 'Who got out the wrong side of the bed?' well, that's a mood hover!

A few other individuals you might want to stay away from include 'Energy Vampires'. With these people, no matter how hard you try to encourage them, show your enthusiasm, or try to give them praise, you will fall flat on your face. No matter how much energy that you put into them, they will suck it out of you like a vampire. If you know of any of these people, avoid them like the plague!

Negative thought processes can exacerbate anxiety. So worrying about what if I lose my job or if I get made redundant or other such situations can lead to just a downward spiral of negative thinking. You're worrying about something that hasn't even happened! Unwarranted fears and doubts can zap all your emotional energy, paralysing you and interfering with daily life. Constant worrying is a heavy burden that will keep you up all night and turn you into a nervous wreck. For chronic worriers, anxiety can be simply fuelled by your own beliefs. If you want to stop worrying and being anxious, then it's important to realise that worrying is the problem in itself. The problem with anxiety is that you can't just switch it off like a tap. You might try distractions but the anxiety will always return.

Write down the anxious thoughts you have on a regular basis. These thoughts need to be placed in the solvable or unsolvable column. Solvable thoughts are normally things that you can do something about in the present, compared to unsolvable problems that are likely to be things that have not actually happened, e.g. a worry that has developed because of a past experience. On a daily basis, have an allocated time slot that will give you the time to reflect and write out what options you have so you are able to have more control of the situation.

Anxious thoughts	Solvable (S) or Unsolvable (US)

From the list of solvable anxious thoughts, I need you to brainstorm your ideas to explore possible solutions, evaluate them by weighing up the pros and cons, and then create an action plan.

With unsolvable worries, think about your emotions towards the situation and accept these feelings as part of being human. You simple have to accept the uncertainties of life. You cannot be absolutely certain about everything in life unless you're psychic! However, is it still reasonable to predict likely outcomes and whether they will be positive, negative or just neutral.

I just need a good night's sleep!!

Sleep is essential. It is something your body needs in order to function. Research proves that, if you suffer from poor sleep patterns, you can develop irrational behaviour, leading to poor judgement and decisions.

Sleep has major impacts on cognitive function and physical and emotional health. The average person needs around eight hours sleep each night. How much sleep do you get on average? One of the consequences of not sleeping regularly is the inability to focus and concentrate for long periods of time. You feel tired and exhausted with reduced spatial awareness, making you less alert. Lack of sleep has also been linked to obesity as chemicals and hormones that play a key role in controlling appetite and weight gain are released when you sleep.

One of the commonest causes of insomnia is stress. Unavoidable stress such as a loved one in hospital or an examination are events that may upset your normal sleep cycle. However, once these challenges are resolved, your normal sleep patterns are likely to return to normal. If you travel abroad regularly for work, then jet lag can also seriously disturb your sleep patterns.

I want you to try these possible solutions as an alternative to medication if you suffer from insomnia or poor sleep patterns.

1. Control the amount of caffeine that you drink throughout the day. These stimulants, including energy drinks, are full of sugar and stimulate you for short periods of time. You will tend to ride the highs and lows of riding a rollercoaster throughout the day as you experience the various surges of energy and no energy. I've seen people live off energy drinks just to keep themselves awake but you are doing more damage to your health physically and mentally than you may think.

2. Keep your bedroom environment dark. When it's time to sleep, this will help the release of melatonin, a hormone that is released by the hypothalamus once the sun goes down. I find the best way to treat a poor sleep cycle is to find out the cause. Once identified, an action plan can be put in place and finally you should ensure some relaxation time for at least an hour before you go to bed.

3. Deep breathing. Try this simple exercise for 5-10 minutes; use your abdomen rather than your chest by inhaling through your nose, pausing for 3-5 seconds then exhaling.

4. One of the things that have really helped me is using lavender oil on my pillow before I sleep. This can help you calm yourself and collect your thoughts before you sleep.

5. To help me relax and deal with stress, a massage is a useful way to iron out tension and knots in your body or, if you prefer, aromatherapy or acupuncture can be just as effective.

6. Regular exercise can improve your sleep pattern, preferably not too close to bedtime. Try to go for a jog or a cycle before you go to work as this will boost your metabolism and stimulate the body.

7. A bedroom is a place to sleep so turning it into your second office or a games room is never a good idea. Move out any laptops, TVs or games machines.

8.	Avoid alcohol. One drink may be fine but alcohol is a diuretic, which means you will want to urinate during the night.

9.	Don't eat after 9pm. If hunger does get the better of you, try to stick to something very light such as a piece of toast. This type of food will release a hormone called serotonin that will help you become sleepy.

10.	Avoid fatty or spicy foods as they could cause heartburn causing discomfort throughout the night.

11.	Create a habit of going to bed and getting up at set times, even at weekends. This will help ensure your body keeps to a regular sleep pattern.

12.	In general, most people tend to have a dip in alertness and energy levels between 2-4pm. If this applies to you, then feel free to take a 10-15 minute power nap!

Physical fitness is not only one of the most important keys to a healthy body, it is the basis of dynamic and creative intellectual activity.

John F. Kennedy

Chapter 2: Making a leap of faith

> *"Your life does not get better by chance,*
> *it gets better by change."*
> **Jim Rohn**

Some people wake up each day in the hope that today is going to have a different outcome or that their life will somehow miraculously transform itself. Unfortunately, this is unlikely to be the case. Your life is in your own hands and you control your own destiny.

Self-esteem or self-worth is simply how you feel about yourself and judge how you are doing in the areas of your life that are important to you. When we have no self-esteem, we tend to generalise, jump to conclusions and find that our lives are full of distortions.

Have you ever been in a situation where you think that someone else does a better job than you? Or that your boss isn't taking sufficient notice of your hard work? These are classic examples of distorted thinking. You need to challenge such generalisations. Ask yourself if they really are doing a better job than yourself and how you know exactly that your boss is not taking any notice of you.

On the following page, I want you to write down a situation where others thought you did something really well. It could have been smashing you monthly sales target, landed a big contract with a client or doing a great presentation. How did that make you feel at that moment?

My page of Big Wins!

Do you ever feel like no one likes you? Then make a list of people that you have shared and enjoyed time with, e.g. at a work night out or an event, such as a wedding you've attended. Would you consider these people as friends? And if they were not your friends, do you think they would have invited you to share those particular moments with you?

I have a great story to tell about one of my clients, David, who used to work in the pharmaceutical industry. From years of training and coaching him, I started to notice a change in his body language, attitude and negative perceptions of life. He was reluctant to discuss his poor mood, but I finally got it out him. He felt that his work was constantly being scrutinised by his new boss. He felt he was being undermined as a professional, resulting in his low self-esteem. His low self-esteem led to a change in behaviour and he started viewing life more negatively, thinking he was useless at everything and any positive successes were just down to pure luck.

As his depressed mood continued to deteriorate, his anxiety levels increased to the point where he hated going to work and he became depressed. His partner and I came up with a strategy to help him snap out of his depressed state. We used counselling and neuro-linguistic programming techniques. He realised that it was no fault of his own that had led him to feel so negatively about his job performance. Instead it was other people who had influenced his self-esteem.

Executives suffering poor self-esteem will tend to find that they don't feel particular important and that their views and opinions are not regarded as relevant. If this is the case, think of the impact your low self-esteem has not only on your own mindset, but also on your work colleagues peers. They may well begin to share your view of yourself! We all have days when you wish you could be somewhere else and that you felt more inspired and accomplished.

On those particular days, do you feel that everyone around you is much cleverer, more attractive and funnier than you, and that you are just a little fish in a big pond? How we see ourselves can often be very different to how others see us. Your perception may be very different because it is based on what you are experiencing or have experienced. This is because you are emotionally attached to these experiences. By removing the emotion, you can change your perception. So imagine you are an angel living in the clouds, looking down on yourself. How does the situation look now? By comparing ourselves with other people and believing what others say about us or imagining what they might say - "They think I'm useless..." or "I'm never going to get that promotion" - you are allowing other people - friends, family, work colleagues, etc. - to decide your level of self-esteem. Your view of yourself is completely subjective. It's not based on true facts.

Activity: We all start to form values and beliefs from a very young age. For example, my values and beliefs include 'help others first and rewards will come later', 'always show gratitude' and 'never allow someone to dictate to you by saying you can't do something or you're not capable of doing it'. What do you value in life and what are your beliefs?

Remember you should be concerned about what you think and not what others think.

Activity: Look in the mirror and think to yourself on a scale of 1-10 how do you feel about yourself right now (1 = I feel terrible to 10 = I love my life and I am unique in every way)? Now write down why do you feel the way you do.

Some of the ways I seek to improve my self-esteem is by writing down my strengths including things such as achievements, skills, accomplishments and things I am good at. This will radically transform your mindset into a more positive one.

You should also write down your weaknesses or those aspects of your life that you would like to improve, e.g. 'I wish I could be more creative' or 'I wish I could manage my time more effectively'. You should then formulate a way to prioritise each particular area using a scale of 1-5. (1 = where you feel something is least important to your life and 5 = the more important). You can then formulate an action plan.

We can do this by asking ourselves some simple questions such as 'you wish to be more creative to do what?' 'What is it about creativity that inspires you?' 'What scenarios or problem-solving methods have you used where creativity was used?' It could have been planning a presentation, for example. You will actually begin to realise that your weaknesses are actually your strengths and that you use them more often or not.

If you're concerned about time management. Then ask yourself: 'If you had more time, what would you do with that extra time?', 'If you could manage time more effectively, what impact would that have on your life?' and 'What strategies have you tried to make your time management more effective?'

Once you are putting the plan into action, you can then start to develop those weaknesses into strengths. By using this process, you will find that your self-confidence will start to grow and you will start to think in a more imaginative style that will help you really begin to find out where your true strengths lie.

> *"Self confidence is the most attractive quality a person can have. How can anyone see how awesome you are if you can't see it yourself?"*
>
> **Unknown**

Most of the business executives that I know have high levels of self-esteem and massive egos. Self-esteem is generally associated with a executive who demonstrates independence and acts very much 'themselves'. As a business leader, you feel like you have great leadership skills and that you're able to give those around you focus and direction and drive the business forward to the best of your abilities. Another great trait is developing and learning how to become more adaptable to meet business and client needs. Your ability to deal with stresses, such as having no time and being under pressure to hit the next sales target, plus the ability to cope with workplace conditions, are all too familiar.

Dealing with these will enhance your mood and help support healthy behaviour and lifestyle. When positive things start to happen, such as improvements to your self-confidence, this will realign you to striving towards what your 'real' self is and what your 'ideal' self is. Executives who build high levels of self-esteem tend to have a positive effect on others. You will feel less anxious about life and in turn more open to change.

Projecting and ensuring a successful self-image within your organisation is vitally important. Your ego represents an internal thought pattern, which is determined by what others think of you and how you act. You can develop a positive ego that can give you lots of benefits. You can use these benefits such as your skills and knowledge to positively impact others and encourage them to aspire to follow you as a good role model. Business professionals that exhibit positive ego have high self-esteem and self-confidence.

The negative ego means you are trying to show everyone who is the best all the time. It's all about you but most of all you're trying to impress and get the attention of the people above. You will do anything in your power to challenge those that get in your way if you feel your ego is threatened. You may think that you will get noticed because you're better than anybody else.

Your work peers will remember you. Ego has its time and place but if you use it too often, you won't be respected and no one likes executives who suck up to their boss. If you use ego all the time, you might feel you get noticed but in reality you're likely to become an insecure, selfish and ignorant person. As a consequence, you will suffer, as you will develop poor self-esteem. Now remember, if you're working long hours just to satisfy your ego, think who suffers? You and your loved ones.

Having high self-esteem and developing a positive ego are generally good responses to a variety of issues, such as stress, organisational change, and changes in your responsibilities or hierarchy. You can help overcome such challenges. This could include improvements to your lifestyle such as weight loss. What you have achieved and how you have achieved becomes part of your life as you live in that moment that becomes an educational journey for you. You will learn and grow through the strategies that worked and that did not work. If you're thinking of embarking on an exercise programme, the questions you need to ask yourself are where you are right now and what you want to achieve by starting an exercise programme.

Now there must be times where you have gazed out of the window whilst sitting on the train as the scenery rushes pass you and you begin to daydream. You're a million miles away! It's great! I recommend that you daydream for at least ten minutes a day. Now that vision could be a mental image. All you need is some clarity to focus on. That image is a little hazy and confusing at the moment but practice daydreaming more and what you want will become crystal clear.

One of the ways to do this is to surround yourself with positive images and even create a vision board or a collage. It will also bring that creative side of your brain that often doesn't get used. For my clients, I ask them to bring in an old picture from when they were particularly happy.

It could be a picture of that beautiful dress which hangs on the wardrobe and it's there when you wake up every day or it could be a dinner suit that you have just purchased for your wedding anniversary. I asked one of my youngest clients, who is a regular footballer, to draw what his dream is and why it is important. He drew a Chelsea football shirt with his favourite number and surname on the back of the shirt. This is what pushes his 'hot button' and gives him the opportunity to focus on something real and tangible. He now believes that he is not just average but better than any other player on the pitch!

Activity: Create a collage of photos or draw an illustration of what you wish to achieve. It could be a collection of images of your family; it could be that next promotion or just an image that has a positive effect on your life.

Motivation is an act or desire to do something in a particular way. It's an internal force that drives people to do particular things. So what motivates you to get up and go to work? What motivates you to give the best presentation to the board of directors on your new business idea? What motivates you to hit your bonus targets for this year? What motivates you to hit this month's sales target? Whatever your motivation, use a scale of 1-10 (1 being 'I don't feel motivated or any sense of urgency or meaning in my life' to a 10 = 'It has positive meaning to my life - I wouldn't miss it for the world' or 'It is the most important thing to me right now').

1. How motivated are you right now to find a good work/life balance?

2. How motivated are you right now to improve your health?

3. How motivated are you to attend your children's sports day (if you have any)?

4. How motivated are you to be promoted at work?

Whatever number you picked, gives your reasons as to why you picked that particular number and not another number.

Knowing how to develop good motivational behaviours in the workplace is essential if you want to be successful. By understanding Herzberg's motivational theory and applying it to your workplace, it will help you understand your motivation and why job satisfaction is not as important as achievement.

How this works is that Herzberg developed the theory that there were two particular factors; one called hygiene factors and the other called motivating factors. He theorised that hygiene factors don't actually motivate you at all. Hygiene factors can be classified as things such as job security, salary, work conditions, policies and procedures, and relationship with subordinates.

However, without these things, or if they are damaged or undermined, we simply don't have a platform to start building our motivating factors. Without our basic hygiene needs being met, we become dissatisfied and unhappy. An example of this could be if the company you work for announces a takeover, the first thing people worry about is job losses. You don't get motivated if your job is under threat but you may work harder.

Motivating factors are related to more job satisfaction, positive motivation, opportunities for personal growth, recognition in the workplace by being taken out for dinner by your boss, your achievements of hitting sales targets and exceeding deadlines.

Once this is in place, this can lead to high motivation, high satisfaction and strong commitment. By understanding your motivating factors, you can then build your own ideas or action plan that will satisfy your own motivating factors.

Story: Sir Ranulph Fiennes is described by the Guinness World Records as 'one of the greatest explorers of his time'. At the age of 65, he set out to climb Mount Everest with his years of training, support and sheer perseverance helping him succeed where others have failed. He had devoted over six years of his life to mountain climbing to overcome his fear of vertigo, which sounds crazy for someone who is a mountain climber. But he used his time to overcome his phobia, gain a world record and raise millions for charity. His motivation was his determination to reach his fundraising targets and desire to overcome his challenges, having previously had double bypass heart surgery.

Another great motivation theory, developed by Abraham Maslow, is the understanding of your basic human needs, or as I like to call them 'qualities'. I have developed a different analogy called Adam's hierarchy of human needs. This is similar but I have adapted it to suit the needs of the business world. There are three main parts to human needs: basic needs, social needs and what I call growth needs.

Basic human needs cover our physiological needs, such as food, water, shelter, warmth, and sex. They include things like job security, the feeling of being safe and secure in your environment, freedom from psychological and physical threats, for example 'the fear of the unknown', protection from excessive criticism, and also the familiarity and stability of routine. These are very similar to the hygiene needs put forward by Herzberg.

The first part of our social needs covers our esteem needs. These relate to self-worth, self-respect, the feeling of your own competence in what you do, and the respect of others. Successful people are full of self-confidence and leadership ability. Driven people like you use ego positively.

The second part of our social needs represents love and a sense of belonging. This is something I really want to elaborate on as many successful business people have no time or choose not to have time for these types of social need. This is about receiving and giving love, affection and trust. Have you ever been in a situation when your wife or partner has said, "Why can't you spend some time with me?" or the impact you have on your children if you get in late from work all the time, making them feel unloved.

Some people go out on expensive shopping trips in order to feel good about themselves. For some people, it helps them to feel loved and get the attention of their partner. Your negative ego is preoccupying your life.

Many successful business people choose to live to work but think who suffers? Why do you think some families suffer breakdown? Because your working life gets in the way. You may feel that because you are working long hours, earning lots of money and earning lots of bonuses, you are doing it for your family but the reality is that you're doing it for yourself and your ego, which is all for the wrong reasons. Let me tell you about your negative ego in more detail because in most circumstances, you will be stuck in a

Adam's Hierarchy of Needs

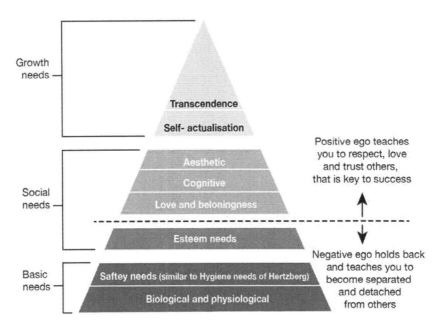

Growth needs

Transcendence

Self- actualisation

Social needs

Aesthetic

Cognitive

Love and beloningness

Esteem needs

Basic needs

Saftey needs (similar to Hygiene needs of Hertzberg)

Biological and physiological

Positive ego teaches you to respect, love and trust others, that is key to success

Negative ego holds back and teaches you to become separated and detached from others

cycle between your esteem needs, and your love and belonging needs. Your major obstacle is your negative ego. Your ego is defined by whom you are as a person and is defined by your toys and possessions. You think that the more you have and the more that you own, you are more valuable as a person.

I knew a client once that lived off her ego and lived a very stressful working life so she frequently went on mad shopping trips buying shoes. The weird thing is in most circumstances she only wore them once or not at all. People with big egos have the need to want more and work harder to get more. They see everyone around them as a threat eventually because they feel others are trying to take everything away from them.

Ego is about you and your achievements and your mind is focused on your successes. You may believe that, if you don't have a big ego, then your reputation will get damaged. Your ego teaches you that you are always right and everyone else around you is wrong: it's your way or no way. There is no compromise with you. The reason why you may not satisfy your love and belonging needs is because your ego teaches you to be separate and detached. By working long hours, you are making that choice so if you want to satisfy these needs, you have to start to live your life on your terms and make choices in your life that don't have detrimental effects on you and your family. If you are a parent, it's vitally important to live up to those responsibilities. Ego is only positive if it's used in a timely manner and not used all the time. Ego can turn negative if it is used all the time.

The third part in the hierarchy of needs is cognitive need. In order to satisfy these needs, you will have the desire to understand and learn. You may read about personal development or watch the Discovery Channel or The Apprentice. The understanding of personal growth is important not just to your working life but also your lifestyle. Personal growth is about learning from your achievements and accomplishments so that you can become a better person.

The next area of need is aesthetic need. In order to satisfy these needs, you may enjoy the outdoors, photography, you may love art, and nature and you will fully appreciate and understand beauty. I satisfy these needs by visiting the local nature reserve and appreciating my surroundings or taking my children to the London Science museum.

The last part of need consists of two parts, which I call growth needs. Self-actualisation is the need to live up to your true potential. Other people's views and opinions don't bother you. You are creative, accepted in society, and spontaneous. You have found your purpose. I believe in giving something back; that's why I have been known for my charity work in the past. This includes raising money for orphans suffering from malnutrition, and football projects in the community. The last area of need is transcendence need, which goes beyond satisfying your own needs. It's about helping others and caring about other people in helping them to self-actualise.

So now you should have an understanding of your own motivational behaviours and needs. Now what you have to do is collectively gather your thoughts and devise an action plan or strategy on how to get motivated.

Your action plan should consist of getting the necessary resources of time, commitment and flexibility. Make a list of things that you are good at and you enjoy. From that I want you to identify a goal that doesn't necessarily need to be massive, but it should help motivate and satisfy your needs.

Once you have identified this goal, write down a risk and reward. A risk is something that you may fear or cause embarrassment to yourself, for example jumping out of a plane or walking into work dressed in the opposite sex's clothes. It could be something you really don't want to do but for others it actually turns into a motivation. A reward could be something really simple such as an evening meal out or a short weekend away.

In order to be truly motivated, you must first start to believe in yourself.

Story: One of the most powerful and moving stories that really bring tears of joy to my eyes is the story of Dick and Rick Hoyt.

Rick was born with a severe neuromuscular disorder leaving him disabled. Doctors said Rick would need to be institutionalised as he would be a vegetable for the rest of his life. The family wanted to take on the responsibility of giving their son a normal life.

At the age of 58, Dick (Rick's father) was told that he was months away from a heart attack. I can't imagine what was going through Dick's mind following this bad news, but his son suggested getting involved with a charity to raise money for other disabled people like him. Dick agreed. Dick's love for his son was huge and he participated in one of the hardest Ironman triathlon events in the southern hemisphere, not on his own but carrying his son Rick every step of the way so that they could share the experience together. He made a special seat on his bike so that Rick could sit down. He made a special dingy so that he could swim and he modified a special buggy so that he could run the gruelling marathon.

It's one of the most moving stories I have ever heard about but the point I'm making is that Dick believed in himself and Rick believed in his father, although everyone around them doubted. Dick and his son are regular participants in Ironman triathlon events all over Australia. Dick and Rick completed a goal that was in most people's eyes impossible.

Trust your feelings. If it feels right, go ahead with all your heart and don't think with your head. It's all gut instinct and having faith in yourself, faith in your goals, faith in your authority and faith in

your ability to change and move forward. The activities and the exercises that I give you in this book will help you empower you to start that journey of change. It's your destiny so trust the journey!! Of course, life has no guarantees so don't criticise before you have even tried it. But if you don't try, you will never know. It will be a case of 'Well, I could've done that, but I didn't'.

Get rid of the excess baggage that means living those old and draining habits. Avoid people that don't stimulate you. Change the environment, either your work environment or home environment.

Get rid of any distractions and eliminate those negative thoughts, they just hold you back. It could be watching TV, hanging out with negative people, or spending too much time on Facebook. Whatever the reason, there will always be an excuse not to do it. My big distraction is my Sony PlayStation.

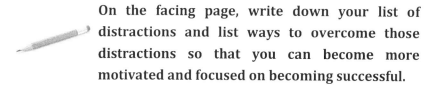

On the facing page, write down your list of distractions and list ways to overcome those distractions so that you can become more motivated and focused on becoming successful.

For example: Reduce time watching TV to spend more time enjoying fresh air. This could help improve cognitive function and oxygen to your brain, thereby enabling greater success that is key for business leaders.

Reduce your working hours (that's outside of work) to take time to meditate. This will help de-junk your mind and tap into your sub-conscious mind to help you relax.

Self-Contract

My goal is:

To achieve my goal, I would need to change the following:

I am willing to do the following to make this happen...

Others will know about the change I'm making when...

If I don't want my plan to work, this is what I'm going to do to make it fail...

Therefore, my contract to myself is

My next tip to get motivated is to tell someone, such as your partner or a work colleague, and find some great supporters. You can recruit some great followers by simply making regular blogs about your progress and asking others how they're getting on. One of the key things is to make up your own self-contract to yourself. Remember a contract means it cannot be broken. But, yes, it can be modified if it has a benefit for you.

Find a buddy who has similar goals and make sure you hold each other to your individual self-contracts. This in turn is very motivating. It brings competition into the process - something which you are very good at.

Stages of change

Before I empower you and show you the solutions to take control of your lifestyle, we must begin to analyse how you are going to change and this can only be done by you. You must ask yourself what mindset you should adopt. Am I ready to make the leap of faith? Am I ready in my mind to change myself and am I going to commit to it? The stages of change model will establish if you are ready to move forward or not. If I haven't convinced you, at least think about how you can embrace change in the next month or two, then I want you to question yourself and ask 'If not now, when?' Because if nothing changes, then nothing changes.

The first stage of change is called pre-contemplation, which in a nutshell means I'm not ready for change and I have no intention in the coming months to change. Really? Well if you're reading this book, then you must be looking to find the solutions that will empower you to take control - so well done! The second stage is contemplation. This basically means that you are in a position where you are thinking about change. So in order to move forward, I urge you to weigh up the pros and cons. For example, if I take up regular exercise then I can lower my blood pressure or, if I go to bed at a sensible time, then I will feel more energetic in the morning. The con could be, if I start exercise, then I might suffer from backache or muscle pain or, if I go to sleep too late, then I will feel exhausted.

Make a list of things that will happen if I don't take action

The third stage is the preparation stage. In this particular stage, you are ready to change or are planning to act very soon. You may have taken steps in the past year to begin this, for example, arranging an appointment with your GP as you were thinking of carrying out an exercise programme, or you visited the local tennis club to enquire about membership. You may need a little more encouragement to make the jump so tell your circle of friends and family about which behaviour you wish to adopt. If you feel you are at this stage, then I would say you are ready to enrol or embark on a programme such as a weight loss or smoking cessation.

The fourth stage is the action stage. So you have made that change and you have carried out the steps that needed to be taken. You will understand that if you have a goal, you will know how to overcome obstacles that could prevent you from achieving your goal. You have taken steps or made changes that prevent relapse.

The fifth stage is the maintenance stage and this is about staying on track and you can do this by reinforcing the risk and reward system. Updating your goals is important as this will keep you interested and build on your self-confidence.

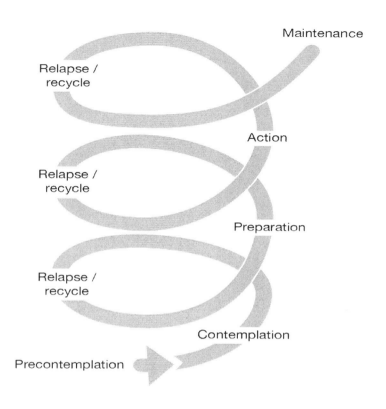

Maintenance

Relapse / recycle

Action

Relapse / recycle

Preparation

Relapse / recycle

Contemplation

Precontemplation

At any point in the stage of change model, anyone can fall back and relapse at any time.

So I really want to help you but you have to want to help yourself!! All of us, including you and me, have procrastinated in our lives. The problem I find with procrastination is that, because you don't have the drive, commitment or determination, you will achieve nothing. Have you ever been in a situation where you have been told in advance to get a report or a business proposal submitted and you leave it to the last minute? Holding yourself back isn't helping. In fact, it makes your life more difficult and places unnecessary stress on you.

In order to embrace change or to make that transition, you must recognise what is disappointing you about your life, and why you want to change. When I speak to clients during a motivational interview to establish their goals, I ask them: "What do you want

to achieve and why do you want to achieve it?" The typical client will say: "I want to lose weight because I need to". After asking numerous other questions and exploring further, I establish that actually they don't want to lose weight but feel they should lose weight because someone made a passing comment. Have you ever felt like that? But actually it may turn out that a client's goals could be something as simple as they just want to have the ability to kick a football and run around with their children, but feel they are not fit enough. They are unhappy with this and don't want to cause embarrassment to themselves and their children. The point I'm making here is there is a higher motivational reason other than just weight loss. So my question to you is what is it that you really want to change in your life? What is it about your mindset, body and lifestyle that disappoints you?

 Let's turn your disappointments into motivations. Make a list of your disappointments on the facing page.

> *"I can accept failure, everyone fails at something. But I can't accept not trying"*
>
> *Michael Jordan*

Choose your destiny and take responsibility to change. We all have choices in life and we all must take accountability. Forget about your old decisions. What's done is done. The choices that you make in your life right now simply do not reflect the way you are today. So make that choice.

In order to choose what life you want to live, you have to have willpower. That means you need fuel to make the engine run. You've really got to want to change and you need to be hungry to accomplish the life you want to its fullest.

Life has its ups and downs, very similar to a rollercoaster, but use those experiences as a learning curve even if you feel it's three steps forward and one step back.

One final tip is to learn from your mistakes you have made in the past and use this to move forward. If something didn't work, don't necessarily disregard it yet. Think how you could modify it or improve your life or situation. Failure is not an option once you have made the profound decision to stick to that decision and not change your mind. It's up to you! The only person that you are letting down is yourself, nobody else.

He who has health,

has hope;

and he who has hope,

has everything.

Thomas Carlyle

Chapter 3: Don't wait until it's too late

Most busy people take their health for granted until eventually it's too late to do anything about it. In the business world, health is often 'put on the backburner' until one day you're told the bad news that could have life-changing consequences. Most of us know somebody - a friend or family members – who have had serious health issues, such as diabetes, coronary heart disease, cancer, stroke, or arthritis, all of which are on the rise. We may be able in some instances to take preventative action through the lifestyles we adopt.

Think of the impact major health problems may have had on the lives of people you know and those around them. Do you want to suffer the same fate? Maybe one or more of the above health issues has affected you. Good health involves not only your physical well-being but your mental well-being as well. So don't gamble with your health: prevention is better than cure. Plus good health gives you more energy, allow you to be more productive and you also become more assertive.

In this particular chapter, I want to help you understand your body, how to assess your current health status and outline ways to improve your health. The health issues discussed in this chapter are commonly associated with people that have to work in high-pressured environments that, in turn, are exacerbated by the lifestyles they live.

Understanding your posture

I've been in the fitness industry for over ten years now and throughout my learning I've been hooked on helping people with their pain issues. The most common reasons why people are in pain is because of poor posture and work issues. I love helping people tackle the root causes of their pain issues, reducing the symptoms they suffer and eventually allowing them to become pain-free. Sitting up straight at one's desk not only projects a good impression, but also more importantly convinces you and others about your good health.

Did you know that at least 80% of people suffer from lower back pain? Adopting a good posture says a lot about you are in terms of your body language, the way you communicate and the importance of opening and closing business deals. It's all to do with how your spine sits on your pelvis. Bad posture is due to the fact that you've sat down for prolonged periods of time, e.g. at your own desk, in meetings or in the car. Your joints begin to stiffen up, you become rigid and you start to slouch as it becomes such an effort to sit or stand up straight. Many thousands of years ago, our ancestors had to hunt for their food in order to survive. Our bodies were not designed to sit down for long periods of time. Subconsciously, we know prolonged sitting is not good for us. Our muscles are insufficiently exercised and can't sustain a healthy posture.

So which posture type are you? The three most common postures I see in my clients are: lordosis, kyphosis and flat back syndrome.

Lordosis is a condition that changes the spine into an exaggerated 'S' curve. Key characteristics include:

1.   Excessive curve in the lower back

2.   Pelvis is tilted under causing the vertebras in lower back to move closer together

3.   Pregnancy or carrying excess abdominal fat

4.   Overworked back muscles

5.   Tight hip flexor (front of the hip) muscles

6. The backs of your legs (hamstrings) are tight

7. Weak core or stomach muscles

8. If you carry a tyre around your mid-section

9. Lower back pain or discomfort

Kyphosis or 'E.T.' position. This condition is called the exaggerated 'C' curve. Key characteristics include:

1. Rounded and tense shoulders

2. Forward head position (your head sits in front of your shoulder line)

3. Neck pain and stiffness

4. Fatigue and low energy levels

5. Sinus issues

6. Pain in the arms

7. Slouching

8. Possibly a hump at the base of your neck. I call this the 'humpback'

Or are you a flat back with a bean pole posture? Key characteristics include:

1. Flattened lower back curve

2. Sciatica (leg pain)

3. Lower back pain especially when sitting for long periods of time

4. Pains in the buttocks, groin or thighs possibly

5. Stiff back

6. Flat bottom syndrome

Understanding the position of your body will affect the position of your spine. Good alignment = good posture. When I observe a client for posture, I look at three viewpoints: anterior (front), side and posterior (back). From the front, I'm looking to check that head, chin, sternum, middle of the pelvis and feet position are all aligned. From the back, I'm looking at the base of the spine, shoulder level, pelvis position, back of the knees and foot structure. And finally the side view focuses on alignment of ear position, shoulder, middle of the elbow, pelvis, knees and feet.

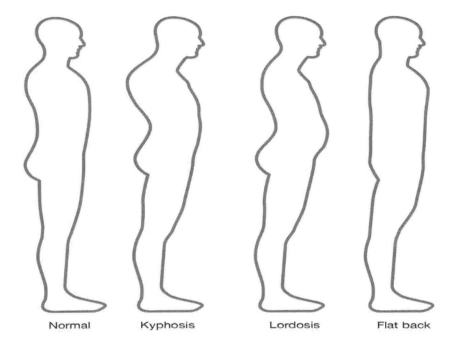

| Normal | Kyphosis | Lordosis | Flat back |

Correcting your posture

There are two ways to correct your posture; through movement (functional exercise) or non-movement, e.g. treatment with a chiropractor.

I'm going to specifically focus on the functional aspect. I believe that poor posture is down to the lifestyle that we choose to adopt and that, in most cases, injuries occur through movement. Some people experience pain from reaching round to grab the seatbelt or leaning over the desk. Functional movement is a great way to improve flexibility, improve joint motion, decrease or eliminate pain, and improve muscular strength. I use this holistic method to get fast and effective results that last.

A functional movement screen should specifically look at three main joints: the hips, foot/ankle and thoracic spine. I regard these joints as having the biggest influence on how we move.

Throughout the assessment I look at improving basic function, i.e. walking or 'gait' and combining observation and experience to also improve posture. Choose your professional wisely. Ideally they should have knowledge about biomechanics, i.e. how the body moves. A professional will train joints, not muscles!!

I get a lot of requests about the 'E.T.' forward-head position. You're probably asking why I call it the 'E.T.' position. In the film 'E.T.', Elliott hides E.T. away from everyone. E.T. stretches his neck out to peak out of the wardrobe. That's what I relate to developing the forward-head position.

This tends to develop because of neck tension, weak back and poor abdominal muscles. The forward head posture then tends to develop a hump at the base of the neck (cervical spine). The head is much heavier than you think; gravity pulls your head down, making the head fall forward. The head's centre of gravity shifts forwards, increasing the muscular effort that is required.

Story: David is 59 years old and has an important role as head of communications. He came to see me because of lower back pain and neck tension.

He was also concerned about his poor posture that led to many aches and pains. His past history revealed that most of his working life involved sitting down at the computer desk. David had severe cervical kyphosis, limited thoracic rotation, lateral flexion and poor thoracic extension.

His medical history revealed that in past years, his posture affected his sinus and ability to breathe correctly.

Now I know that some people will think, "Well, I'll just take a pain-killer or visit the GP and the pain will go away". Unfortunately, this is not the case. You have to deal with the cause, not the symptoms (Cohen, JS. 2001). Here are some great tips to help you improve your posture.

1.   Adjust your driving position. It's amazing but by simply adjusting your seat position, you can have a dramatic effect on your posture, especially if you regularly drive lots of miles. Do you remember when you were learning to drive? Do you remember the driving instructor asking you never to sit too close to the wheel or too far away? If you have your face practically against the windshield or sit leaning back, then you need to make an adjustment. The steering wheel should be at arm's length. The seatback doesn't have to be vertical, but in a position that supports your head. The top of the steering wheel needs to be at eye level.

2.   In the office. If you sit a lot at your desk, adjust your chair position by making sure the chair is the correct height for the keyboard or desk, making sure the chair fully supports your back and keeping the chair close to the desk in order to prevent the need to reach forwards.

3.   Move around. Your body was designed to move, not for sitting. Go for a walk around the office briefly every 90 minutes to help mobilise your joints.

By making these simple adjustments, you will improve your posture, you'll also improve your digestive process and how the body efficiently transports vital nutrients, giving you more energy! By making these adjustments, you put less pressure on other parts of the body and strengthen the muscles that help support the joints and aid movement. You will also find that you will be generally less fatigued and more alert. You'll feel better!

Irritable bowel syndrome

Irritable bowel syndrome (IBS) is a digestive condition. It can cause bouts of stomach cramps, bloatedness, diarrhoea and constipation. It can be terribly uncomfortable and embarrassing when you want to go to the bathroom and are unable to because it causes too much pain and discomfort. If you suffer from IBS, it can either feel like you going to toilet and pushing a brick through or running to the toilet every 5 minutes. Not only that, but with constipation you will be irregular and often have bloody stools. This may happen due to the fact your diet is generally poor and lacking in vital nutrients. In some cases, it may indicate that you have a food allergy, such as gluten or wheat intolerance. If you are highly stressed, you tend to neglect your body. This can often lead to a disruption of normal function. Dehydration is very common for people who suffer from these common digestive issues. Drinking lots of tea and coffee doesn't count. Research tells us that the cause of IBS is unknown. However, studies have suggested that stress and digestion go hand in hand.

Use this checklist to help alleviate some of your symptoms

1.   Eat more dark green vegetables, such as cabbage, broccoli and courgettes

2.   Incorporate healthy oats, nuts and bran into your diet

3.   Drink at least 1.5 - 2 litres of bottled or filtered water daily

4.   Avoid fruit juices (especially the concentrated juices). The sugar content may irritate the digestive tract. Fruit juices are also calorific

5.   Incorporate probiotics into your diet. These are the healthy bacteria found in your gut that help keep your stomach healthy and in harmony. These can be found in products such as yogurts

High blood pressure - 'the silent killer'

In the business world, did you know that 80% of executives and an estimated one billion people worldwide suffer from high blood pressure (hypertension)? Hypertension is responsible for an estimated 45% of deaths across the globe due to heart disease and stroke. I refer to high blood pressure as the "silent killer" as there are often no warning signs or symptoms. The causes are down to the high amounts of sodium we ingest from processed meats and foods and a sedentary lifestyle. Research suggests that highly pressured environments increase stress levels, which can lead to high blood pressure. Blood pressure is simply the pressure of the blood against the walls of the veins and arteries. If you suffer from high blood pressure, then you increase the chances of a heart attack or stroke or the long-term effects of coronary heart disease (CHD). If you suffer from regular headaches, migraines, dizziness, high anxiety levels and poor sleep, then these are clear signs that you may have high blood pressure. Smoking, excessive drinking, obesity and diabetes can also cause high blood pressure.

My advice is getting yourself checked out as a precaution. If you are thinking of embarking on an exercise programme, consult with your GP first or ask a personal trainer. Alternatively, you can check your blood pressure yourself. Most pharmacies have automatic blood pressure monitors called sphygmomanometer available for purchase. Place the blood pressure cuff around the top part of your right arm and tighten with the provided straps (but not too tight). Turn your hand so your palm is facing upwards and relax your arm, ideally resting it on a table. Press the activation button. This should inflate the cuff and after 30 seconds or so, it should give you a reading.

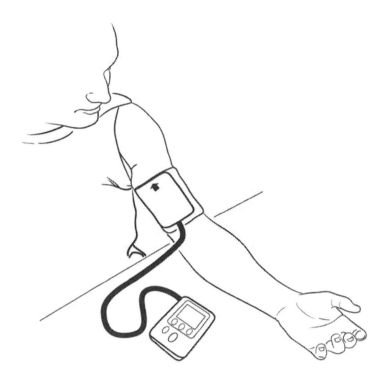

The first reading is normally the high one (systolic). This is the maximum force that the blood flows from the heart whilst beating into the arteries. It should not read higher than 130 mmHg. The second reading (diastolic) is the force as the heart relaxes, allowing blood to flow back to the heart. This should not read higher than 90 mmHg. If it does, double-check and make sure you've followed the procedure correctly. Ask your GP if you need a second opinion. The best time to measure your blood pressure is first thing in the morning, ideally before you eat anything and you are in a relatively relaxed state. If you measure your blood pressure on a regular basis, then make sure you do it at the same time of day.

Blood pressure can be improved by integrating interval training (exercise) for a minimum of 20-30 minutes at least three times a week. An example of this could be 5 minutes of fast walking followed by 5 minutes of light jogging then 5 minutes of steady running and repeat. Give yourself some variety so it keeps you interested and makes it more fun.

Metabolic syndrome/ insulin resistance

I can best describe metabolic syndrome as the precursor state prior to being diagnosed with type 2 diabetes. If you regularly consume sugary foods and drinks, it puts the pancreas under severe pressure as it is overworked. The pancreas releases insulin to balance blood sugar levels. This is to keep the body within normal homeostasis (normal body function). If you consume, for example, your favourite milk chocolate bar or a ripe banana, your body will turn this into glucose. The higher the amount of glucose that is released, the higher the spike in blood sugar. If you have high blood sugar levels, you may have lots of energy for a short space a time, whereas with low sugar you tend to have no energy. You will want to fall asleep and you feel fatigued all the time. If you suffer from metabolic syndrome, then you may develop insulin resistance meaning that the pancreas becomes less efficient in releasing insulin at the right time. You can minimise your risks of metabolic syndrome using a low glycaemia diet. We are going to explore this further in the book together with other steps you can take for a healthy lifestyle. If you carry a tyre around your mid-section, then there is a chance that you may also be exhibiting the symptoms of metabolic syndrome. Diabetes is a life-changing condition and, once you have it, there is no getting rid of it. It stays with you for the rest of your life.

Some of the classic symptoms of metabolic syndrome include

1. Obesity and abdominal fat: more often or not, your appearance gives this away. Your body shape is basically shaped like an 'apple'.

2. High blood pressure: this could include dizzy spells, regular headaches, shortness of breath and blurred vision.

3. High cholesterol: this is when fat clogs up your arteries. Completing a simple blood test with your GP can test this.

4. High blood sugar levels: by testing your blood sugar levels regularly, you can monitor the amount of sugar in the bloodstream. A simple pinprick test to monitor this can be done through your GP, or ask your pharmacist for options. Regular exercise can help regulate sugar levels more effectively by burning up excess sugar levels and helping you to burn fat.

5. Gout: if you suffer from regular gout, this is the classic sign of high sugar levels. Gout includes swelling, inflammation of the ankles, wrists and other joints. Gout can be very painful and uncomfortable. Tenderness, redness and pain are common.

I'm going to give your lifestyle 'first aid' and show you how to achieve the perfect body.

The point I'm making with regards to your health is that it should be a top priority: where would you be without your health? You can't earn as much money, you can't be as successful and you can't be as competitive. Your health affects you, not just physically but mentally as well.

Chapter 4: The balancing act

In this particular chapter, we are going to explore who you are today (your current real self) and how to achieve your ideal self (the person in the future). The real self is described as who you are today in the present. It is about the way you feel about yourself when you look in the mirror. What do you see? Do you feel tired and fatigued, or full of energy? How do you feel your life is going right now? Do you love your life, or do you feel like you are letting others down?

Understanding your real self is about understanding the way you look. Are you happy with the way you look? If you look in the mirror, what do you see? How do you compare how your look? What is the best way that describes the way you look?

The real self also consists of describing the way you think. Do you need direction, or do you like to lead? Do you need more knowledge, or want to share more knowledge? Do you think by working long hours you are making your family happy?

How do you feel about the way you act? Do you feel like people see you as too serious or someone that can have a laugh with? How do you act around work colleagues and your family? Do you act differently? If so, how and why?

As you can see, there are lots of questions to ask yourself.

On the following page, write down in as much detail how you feel, look, think and act around people. From your perspective, also describe your personality. Are you an introvert or extrovert? Are you a good listener, outgoing, competitive, and approachable? Whatever it is, write it down.

The ideal self is someone that you want to be. It is an image that you have developed over a period of time. From your life experiences, you will begin to evaluate what you have learned from life.

To help you create that image, I want you to think of someone that you admire. It could be a player from your favourite football team that you support, it could be a politician, a celebrity, an entrepreneur, your boss or a family member.

In as much detail as possible, write down on the following page what you admire about them most. What do you see that others don't? Why do you admire them? Is it their fame and fortune, or how ruthless they are in the boardroom, or how caring they are towards others?

One of the people I most admire is Sir David Attenborough. The main reason for this is I love his appreciation and understanding of nature. His knowledge has helped preserve endangered species and increase awareness of how our ever-changing planet is having an impact on animals today. This gives me the drive to want to learn more about how I can help preserve our planet for our future descendants - and realign my real self to my ideal self of the future.

Now looking back at what you have written down about yourself and your personality. How does it compare to the person you most admire? How far are you from achieving that ideal self? What can you do to make improvements to get within reach of achieving your ideal self?

If you want to move towards positive growth, you must first develop a healthy mind and be very clear about what you need to achieve that.

Here are some fantastic strategies that can be used to improve your 'Ideal self'

1. First make a 'commitment' to yourself and be committed to achieving your objective

2. Establish your reasons why you feel the way you do

3. Understand what you need to do in order to change yourself

4. Believe in yourself

5. Set goals

6. Have a support group

When we establish in our minds what our ideal self needs to look like, it must be related to our core values in life. Below is another activity to help you understand those values and beliefs and why living life by those values is important to you as a person.

1. Who is the person that you most respect in your life? What are their core values?

2. Who is your best friend and what are their key qualities?

3. If you could have one more career orientated quality, what would it be and why?

4.   What are your 'pet hates'?

5.   What compliments do people most often give you?

6.   What are the three most important values that you want to pass onto your children?

7.   If you were given the opportunity to counsel a group of students about to graduate, what advice would you give them?

8.   What are your 'Top 3' values in life?

Examples of my top values that I always speak about to my children is that family comes first, be honest and open, and try your hardest and never give up.

Chapter 5: Achieving work/life balance

Y ou will have your own perspective of what constitutes a good work/life balance. For me, personally, I believe it is about balancing my working life with the things that I enjoy in life. One of the things I love to do is spend good quality time with my children and share their achievements and experiences. It gives you a sense of being a proud parent and reflects my core values.

Another view of work/life balance is the concept of prioritising your lifestyle (health, pleasure, leisure, family and spiritual development) together with your work life, e.g. career and ambition. The clients that I work with often feel that their career should be their number one priority and not their family. Well this is the wrong approach.

Some people dread going home to their partners because they don't want to be nagged for working long hours. Ironically, they believe that, by working these ridiculous hours, they are doing it for them. I want to give you a reality check: you're not working these long hours for them, you are doing it for yourself!! To satisfy your ego!!

I'm going to show you a very effective way to evaluate your work/ life balance using the 'Circle of Success'. There are no correct or incorrect answers and nobody is going to judge you. This is for your eyes only! It will help identify how balanced your life really is and it will highlight areas where you could improve the balance. Be honest and truthful with your answers and you will get the most out of this exercise.

Circle of Success

Relationships and family	Please circle the most appropriate answer
I can easily trust those that I live and work with	1 2 3 4 5
I recognise the need for support and am continually seeking help	1 2 3 4 5
I spend at least 10 hours on focused family time each week	1 2 3 4 5
I get together with friends at least once a week	1 2 3 4 5
I'm actively engaged in ways to support friends and family, and help encourage them to be successful	1 2 3 4 5
I take complete responsibility for relationship conflicts should they arise	1 2 3 4 5
It is easy for me to make commitments and honour them	1 2 3 4 5
I'm actively engaged in learning on how to be a better spouse, parent and/or friend	1 2 3 4 5
I'm 100% honest and open with those that live and work with me	1 2 3 4 5
I get very jealous if others achieve things before I do	1 2 3 4 5
	Total

Work and career	Please circle the most appropriate answer
My goals are written down, displayed and regularly reviewed	1 2 3 4 5
I love what I do and look forward to the next working day	1 2 3 4 5
I'm filled with a sense of accomplishment and achievement	1 2 3 4 5
I'm consistently trying to improve on my strengths and weaknesses	1 2 3 4 5
I am at home with the family on time every day	1 2 3 4 5
I plan my days at least a week in advance	1 2 3 4 5
I am good at delegating tasks and activities	1 2 3 4 5
My team look at me as a great leader and role model	1 2 3 4 5
I work in a positive environment	1 2 3 4 5
I don't feel like my work deadlines and targets are unrealistic	1 2 3 4 5
	Total

Financial	Please circle the most appropriate answer				
I save at least 10% of my income every month	1	2	3	4	5
My credit cards are debt free	1	2	3	4	5
I have a set-aside fund to last me six months	1	2	3	4	5
I feel that I am paid according to my value and worth	1	2	3	4	5
I have a will and testament just in case the inevitable should happen	1	2	3	4	5
I live well below my means and never spend money irresponsibly	1	2	3	4	5
I have completed a detailed budget and stick to it	1	2	3	4	5
I have a range of investments, stocks and shares	1	2	3	4	5
I have a financial plan in place for my retirement	1	2	3	4	5
I have a range of pension plans that I can get access to on my retirement	1	2	3	4	5
	Total				

Spiritual	Please circle the most appropriate answer
I would consider myself a spiritual person	1 2 3 4 5
I take at least 15 minutes each day to meditate and reflect on my life	1 2 3 4 5
Other people that come into contact with me would consider me spiritual	1 2 3 4 5
I study my spiritual beliefs on a daily basis	1 2 3 4 5
I practise my spiritual beliefs on a daily basis	1 2 3 4 5
I am dedicated to growing as a person using my spiritual beliefs	1 2 3 4 5
I use my knowledge in spirituality to resolve my problems	1 2 3 4 5
I use my spirituality to help and advise others	1 2 3 4 5
I use visualisation daily to help me relax and live life	1 2 3 4 5
I have a strong belief in faith	1 2 3 4 5
	Total

Mental well-being	Please circle the most appropriate answer				
I read inspirational material to help my personal development for at least 30 minutes each day	1	2	3	4	5
I listen to inspirational material to help my personal development for at least 30 minutes each day	1	2	3	4	5
I have a mentor that I trust	1	2	3	4	5
All of my friends are a positive influence in my life	1	2	3	4	5
I visualise achieving my goals and objectives	1	2	3	4	5
I'm always smiling	1	2	3	4	5
I reflect on what I'm grateful for every day in my life	1	2	3	4	5
I have purpose in my life	1	2	3	4	5
I always say no to any requests or obligations that don't fit my core values and beliefs	1	2	3	4	5
I don't feel insecure in my life	1	2	3	4	5
	Total				

Lifestyle	Please circle the most appropriate answer
I have hobbies that I enjoy and I spend time on them at least three times a week	1 2 3 4 5
I take a holiday at least once a year without any work communication	1 2 3 4 5
I spend as much time as I want with my family	1 2 3 4 5
I spend as much time as I want with friends	1 2 3 4 5
I feel there is enough time in the day to balance both work and family life	1 2 3 4 5
I live life to its fullest every day	1 2 3 4 5
I attend cultural events at least twice a month, e.g. museums, opera, carnivals, concerts, etc.	1 2 3 4 5
I love adventure and I'm always looking for the next new experience	1 2 3 4 5
I have a 'bucket' list of the places I wish to explore	1 2 3 4 5
I support events that friends and family take part in	1 2 3 4 5
	Total

Relationships and family	Please circle the most appropriate answer
I do a mixture of cardiovascular training at least three times a week	1 2 3 4 5
I do strength training at least three times a week	1 2 3 4 5
I regularly attend either Yoga and/or Pilates classes three times a week	1 2 3 4 5
On an average day, I spend no more than one hour watching TV	1 2 3 4 5
I have a filling breakfast before I leave the house (not just a hot drink)	1 2 3 4 5
I don't ever eat ready-meals or microwave dinners	1 2 3 4 5
I spend at least 30 minutes outdoors daily	1 2 3 4 5
I don't ever eat fast-food takeaways	1 2 3 4 5
I have at least eight hours of uninterrupted sleep daily	1 2 3 4 5
I'm not a regular binger drinker	1 2 3 4 5
I drink at least the equivalent of eight glasses of water daily	1 2 3 4 5
	Total

To determine the balance of your life, take all of your scores and plot them on the clock on the following page. You must start from the centre and use the key to mark your current status. Then connect all the dots within the clock to see how much balance you have in your life. If there are serious deviations or flat spots, then you will know what areas of your life you need to work on.

Key:

Score of 5   1 notch

Score of 6-10   2 notches

Score of 11-15   3 notches

Score of 16-20   4 notches

Score of 21-25   5 notches

Score of 26-30   6 notches

Score of 31-35   7 notches

Score of 36-40   8 notches

Score of 41-45   9 notches

Score 46-50   10 notches

Please use the same score for family and relationships.

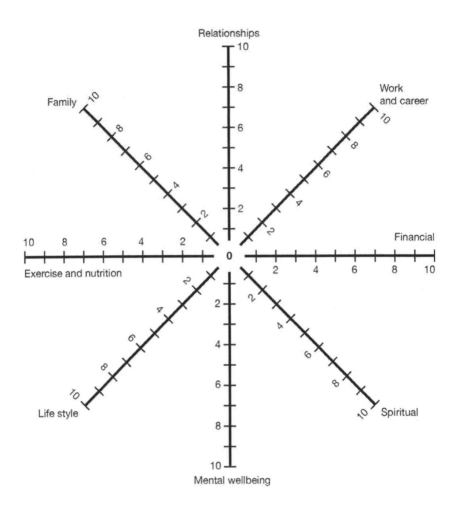

I believe one of the key ways to get balance into your life is to have a good laugh. Laughter is powerful as it uses facial muscles in your face that don't get used very often. Have you ever been to a comedy club and you walked out and your cheekbones were aching? If you don't laugh that often, then smile. A great exercise to help you smile, especially first thing in the morning, is to visualise a time in your life that made you smile or laugh. It could have been an embarrassing night out. It could have been the birth of your child. It could be that you remember a comedian's joke on TV. Whatever it is, write it down.

What makes you smile? If you start your day with a smile, it will determine the type of day that you are likely to have and put you in a more positive place. This positivity will rub off on others in your team too.

So did that help you understand your life balance? Did the Circle of Success surprise you in any way? And do you think there are areas that you need to look at more closely to create a good work/life balance?

Time management is an art

One of the key main areas to being an effective leader is having great time management skills. This is an art that some executives find very hard. I'm sure that you have been in a conversation with a friend, family member or business acquaintance and they ask you, "How is life treating you?" or "Can you complete this report or hit this sales target by the end of the week?" I know what you're thinking - "Not enough hours in the day". We've all been there. Developing effective time management skills takes time, experience and knowledge to achieve. I'm going to show you the tools to develop this skill.

Plan holidays in advance: living your life comes first and the best way to plan is to book your holidays in advance. The best way to do this is to purchase a big wall planner and make sure it has all the public holidays, including Christmas and Easter, on it. If you have children, make a list of all their school holidays. Commit to those dates and take the allocated holiday time. I always find that even a long weekend away is great way to recharge my batteries.

Effective time management starts with your diary. Ideally have two; one paper, the other electronic. Using a diary is a great way to plan so use it for things like attending your children's sports day, attending the gym, and business appointments. Whatever it is, stick it in.

I'm going to be talking about goals later but having goals is very important as they give you purpose, focus and direction. An action plan is key to strategising. It will guide you to achieve your goals and objective/s, and set out when you are going to achieve them by.

Feeling overwhelmed with not enough time can be quite common. My advice is to get into the office early by 10 minutes. By getting in early, you don't fall behind your schedule and cause yourself unnecessary stress. So start with the small changes that can make a big difference.

Sometimes it's hard to delegate because you feel that you have been given that task and you want to complete it to your own high standards and the expectations of others. You believe that you are the only one that can do the task. One of the key qualities to being a successful leader is to trust in your belief in others. If you feel that someone else could do a particular task to a high standard, then delegate it to them. By putting trust in others, you empower them and build successful relationships. We should all understand that everyone has the same 24 hours as everybody else.

This is the key to time management - to see the value of every moment.

Menachem Mendel Schneerson

A muscle is like a car.
If you want it
to run well
early in the
morning,
you have to
warm it up.

Florence Griffith Joyner

Chapter 6: The Lifestyle Strategy

The first part of developing a lifestyle strategy is to establish your goals. To have a goal, you simply need to have purpose, focus and motivation in achieving that objective. I'm sure you have been given work targets before. Well setting your personal goals is just like setting your work targets. In this chapter, I'm going to show you a simple way to set your goals and a simple formula to achieve them. But before we do that, I'm going to give you some very simple guidelines on how to write you goals.

> ## "Goals are the fuel in the furnace of achievement"
>
> ### Brian Tracy

1. Don't just think about your goals, write them down. Writing down your goals is key as otherwise they may get 'lost in translation' as new issues and situations arise in your life. So don't get distracted: write each goal down straight away.

2. Suspend reality. Take a step out and detach yourself from the current reality of your world. Right now, if you had every resource, ability and skill imaginable, what would you do with these assets? How could you make your life better than it is today? What could you accomplish and whom could you influence? Don't hold back: don't allow your current abilities and skills to limit you. Allow your thoughts and imagination to transcend reality! At this point, you should be simply brainstorming ideas. You don't need to start committing to anything or writing down goals. Have you ever read or watched 'Aladdin'? The genie has the power to grant three wishes. Well, I'm going to let you have ten! So go for it and write down your ten wishes.

3. Give yourself permission to think and dream as big as you want. If you could guarantee success at the end of the journey, what would you go for? What's your life's big ambition, or what have you always wanted to do? What is the one outrageous goal that makes you sweat at the palms and increases your heart rate? What gives you that surge in adrenalin?

> *"We all have dreams. But in order to make dreams come into reality, it takes an awful lot of determination, dedication, self-discipline, and effort"*
>
> *Jesse Owens*

4. Stay positively focused by deciding what you want to move towards, not away from. I find visualisation helps me with this exercise. Examples of positive visualisation could include: 'I am my ideal weight of 72 kg by April next year' rather than 'I lose 10 kg by April next year"; or 'I am a great parent' versus 'I am a better parent'.

5. Visualise yourself as how you want to be by saying 'I am' rather than 'I want to be'. This will help you switch on the creative side of your brain as you have declared how you visualise yourself. Doing this empowers you to become whom you say you are.

6. Be sure to really own your goals:

A goal is just a wish unless it is written down

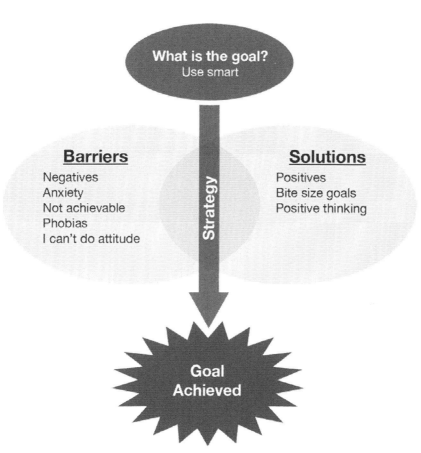

Many people set goals because they feel they are the types of goals they ought to aspire to rather than what they really want for themselves. Don't let friends, family, works peers or social pressures dictate to you what you should dream and desire. Your goals need to come from your heart and your inner self. By not setting yourself goals that are really your own, you will not really believe you are capable of achieving them and most likely fail to meet them because they are something that you didn't really want anyway.

Now I want you to write down and list your goals from each of the eight priority areas of your life. You are not being held accountable at this point. We will come to that later. Whatever comes up in your mind, write it down. You don't necessarily have to fill in all eight priority areas, but try to fill in as much as you can.

Business

This could include things such as planning and reviewing your career/work goals on a regular basis, improving team development, finding a coach, or hitting certain sales targets, etc.	
1.	2.
3.	4.
5.	6.
7.	8.

Financial

These could include beginning an investment plan, paying off your credit cards, setting up a high interest savings account, organising a will, saving for your children's university fees, setting up a private pension, or arranging charity giving, etc.

1.	2.
3.	4.
5.	6.
7.	8.

Physical

This could include running a marathon, improving your flexibility, improving your posture, reducing your blood pressure, making an appointment with your GP, reducing fried fatty foods in your diet, reducing alcohol consumption, cutting down on caffeine, or working with a personal trainer, etc.

1.	2.
3.	4.
5.	6.
7.	8.

Mental

This could include reading personal development and growth books, positive visualisation, hiring a coach, managing your time more effectively, developing a vision board, etc.	
1.	2.
3.	4.
5.	6.
7.	8.

Family

This might include spending more time with the family, make sure your home for dinner with the family, planning outings, reading bedtime stories to your children, etc.	
1.	2.
3.	4.
5.	6.
7.	8.

Spiritual

This might include: attending church more regularly, meditating or exploring spiritual or religious beliefs, etc.	
1.	2.
3.	4.
5.	6.
7.	8.

Lifestyle

This might include travelling, exploring where you would like to live, identifying people you would like to meet, spending time on hobbies, developing foreign language skills, taking up adventure activities, learning a musical instrument, cutting back on business travel, etc.

1.	2.
3.	4.
5.	6.
7.	8.

Relationships

This might include remembering to send birthday cards to friends and family, stopping or limiting contact with negative people, spending time with close friends, planning breaks away with a partner, identifying people you would like to get know more, putting photos of your family on your desk, etc.

1.	2.
3.	4.
5.	6.
7.	8.

Top ten: Now we need to sort out and prioritise your top ten goals from the list above. Use this checklist to define your top ten goals. This will help you narrow them down from the lists above. Put a letter against each category, e.g. R = relationship, then your goal, the date by when you are going to reach the goal, and the risks and rewards in achieving the goal.

Category	Goal	Deadline	Risk	Reward

Category	Goal	Deadline	Risk	Reward

> *"Without goals and plans to reach them, you are like a ship that has set sail with no destination"*
>
> *Fitzhugh Dobson*

Setting goals the 'smart way'

I'm sure you have seen this before, but I think this is a very simple way of constructing goals. I'm sure you're probably already very familiar with using the S.M.A.R.T. method when setting business goals or working in team meetings.

S = Specific: this means the goal is clear, defined and recognisable to anyone.

An example could be 'I want to lose 5 kg in weight within two months' versus just 'I want to lose weight'.

M = Measurable: measuring your progress is very important and motivating as it helps you stay on track, reach your target dates and experience the importance of accomplishing goals or each individual step ('little wins'). Measurement helps drive you to continuing your efforts towards achieving your goals. In order to measure a particular goal, ask yourself questions, such as 'How will I know once I've achieved it?'

An example of measurable goals are 'I want to achieve a blood pressure level of less than 130/90' or 'I want to reduce my cholesterol to below 5.5' versus simply saying 'I want to get healthy'.

A = Attainable or Achievable. Try not to live in the clouds with your goals. For example, you're not going to solve world hunger by the end of the month or lose half your body weight by the end of the week. Don't just rely on sheer luck to achieve your goal. It won't happen without your commitment and effort.

R = Relevant. Make sure that your goals relate to the core beliefs you wrote down earlier. Your goals must be aligned to the vision you have of your life and what you want to get out of it.

T = Timely. I'm sure that every day and week, you have deadlines that you need to meet. Achieving your goals should be realistic but also an exciting challenge. You need to be in a position to step up to the challenge. Leaders like you excel at challenges. While you need sufficient time to achieve the goals you set yourself, you should be hungry to accomplish them.

Now finally, you need to make sure your goals are 'balanced'. You should review your ten goals and make sure that they represent each area of your 'Circle of Success'. With lifestyle strategy, the grand goal is to achieve success in every area of your life. Don't end up as the person with a 20-room mansion in the country, but no family to share it with, or the guy in the gym with big muscular arms and weak, skinny legs.

What you get by achieving your goals is not as important as what you become by achieving your goals

Zig Ziglar

Exercise is the catalyst.
That's what makes everything
happen: your digestion, your
elimination, your sex life, your
skin, hair, everything about you
depends on circulation.
And how do you
increase circulation?

Jack LaLanne

Chapter 7: Move it or Lose it

Movement is an important part of the lifestyle strategy. Humans were engineered and designed to move. Millions of years ago, our ancestors had to hunt animals, forage for roots and berries, and basically live off the land in order to survive. In industrial age, people still had to perform labour-intensive tasks such as mining and manufacturing. Now as we move into the information age, our lifestyle and job habits have changed remarkably as manufacturing and productions increasingly rely on machines and computers rather than the physical strength of people.

Society today is now full of convenience shopping and technology. We are becoming smarter but also physically lazier. So many of us in the business world live virtually an entirely sedentary lifestyle in the workplace: long periods of time sitting down and staring at a screen. This lifestyle is leading to weight gain, poor posture and other health problems for more and more people. It's not just our physical health either. Our lifestyles can often lead to psychological issues, such as depression. The fewer physical demands on our bodies, the less capable our muscles and vital organs become in doing their job properly.

It is so easy to convince yourself that there is not enough time in the day to fit exercise into your life. This particular chapter will examine the best ways to introduce exercise into your busy life, the secrets to achieving quick results in the least time possible and provide you with the inspiration to get your body moving. You will quickly realise both the physical and mental benefits of exercise and how exercise something you simply cannot live without. So my advice is to get up and MOVE around. The human body is a remarkable machine so use it!

Every 90 minutes or so, go for a quick stroll, even if it's just around the office, or go outside and breathe in some fresh air. It's amazing how you can lift your mood and energy levels by performing these simple activities. This will help increase the mobility and flexibility of the joints, which is very important since this is something we tend to lose quite rapidly as we age. Additionally, these types of activity will help reduce the risk of injuries from everyday movements that we take from granted, such as putting on your seat belt on or picking up a bag of groceries. Another big bonus is that you will lose body fat more naturally even when you're not involved in any formal exercise programmes or sports. You will also begin to fully appreciate your body in a different light from the way you look and feel. If you don't use it, you will simply lose it!

From my years of experience of working in gyms, it frustrates me to see so many people still relying on fixed resistance machines. Just think about it: you have been sitting down most of the day, so do you really think you are going to get any results or stimulation by performing meaningless tasks by sitting at an exercise machine on your backside? I hope your answer will be the same as mine - 'NO'!

Functional training or, as I like to call it, purposeful training is a great way to get started as it often mimics natural movement patterns and functions that we take for granted on a daily basis. Have you ever been in a situation where you have leaned across the desk, bent down to get something or reached out in order to get to something and suddenly out of nowhere you get a sharp pain in your lower back? By engaging in a functional training programme, you will get faster results, you will burn calories more efficiently, and you're less likely to suffer from those aches and pains.

Exercise One: back squats (if you suffer from back issues then turn your toes in slightly to activate more gluteal muscles).

Exercise Two: lunge in different directions (repeat the same lunge in each directions of the compass - North, South, East and West, followed by North East, North West and South East and South West.

Exercise Three: press-ups (try a few variations with hands positioned square, wide or narrow.

Most of my clients that I work with come from the corporate world and I always spend the last fifteen minutes doing what I like to call 'frustration training'. I'm talking about boxing training! Have you ever watched a boxing match? It is really hard work but it offers the potential for you to increase your fitness levels two-fold. Have you ever shaken a soft drink can really hard and when you pull the clip, it explodes? Well, when you engage in boxing training, it releases all that adrenalin and pushes your body to its limits. It will not only boost your self-confidence, but also enable you to better address challenges and perform at a much higher standard.

Have you ever been in a situation, especially in the gym, where you have developed a routine? You begin to see results initially, but then no matter how hard you work, your body shape doesn't change. Performing slow long-duration exercises is simply counter-productive and quite pointless frankly. The cortisol levels (stress hormones) increase significantly and this often leads to frustration and poor exercise adherence. Interval training is the most efficient way to burn body fat as you can often maximise your workout by burning more calories in shorter space of time.

Examples:

15 minutes on the rower (2 minute warm up followed by 1 minute medium pace, 1 minute fast pace and then 1 minute slow pace)

Running, jogging or brisk walking: 2 minutes warm-up, followed by 1 minute of light jogging, 1 minute of brisk walking followed by 1 minute of medium-pace running followed by 3-second sprints. Repeat for 20 minutes.

I suggest using an exercise intensity scale of 1-10 (1 = very low intensity. 10 is where you are pushing yourself to your limit). This method is called Rate of Perceived Exertion (RPE). Using the RPE scale, you can simply perform and maximise your workout more effectively to the intensity suited to your needs.

Warm up: RPE of 3-5

Main session: 6-9

Cool down: 2-5

In order to stay on the path of change, you must be consistent in what you do. It's easy to become inconsistent. Have you ever set a New Year's resolution and said to yourself: 'I will drop a waist size by the end of the month', or 'I will not drink any alcohol during January'? But how many days does it take before you break that promise to yourself?

How would you like to be in the privileged minority that does follow through and stick to your promises? Most people initially get the results they want, but often they get distracted, prioritising what they perceive as more important issues. Being consistent will increase exercise adherence and raise your belief levels. Why wait until the New Year to make the decision? Why not now?

Working out at the right time is very important. It will all depend on what time of day works better for you. Some of you will tend to work out in the morning and this often sets you up for the day by giving your metabolism the kick-start that is needed. Or if you're like me, you may prefer to exercise towards the end of the day. But whatever time you choose, make sure it feels right and works for you.

One of the key components of achieving your goals is a structured training programme. Having the right structured training programme is ultimately very important and is frankly essential in ensuring you get the results you want. Really knowing what weights, duration and order of exercises and intensity levels are some of the key factors you need to take into consideration when you're planning your programme. In a short space of time, you will want to take it up a level and you will begin to question if your exercise programme is effective or not. By investing in a good quality personal trainer, you can accelerate those results because they are the experts in achieving wonders. If that's not an option, ask a gym instructor or class instructor for their advice. Don't feel embarrassed or intimated, most people don't reach their potential because they're afraid of asking. Fitness professionals can accelerate your results and help you achieve them in the shortest space of time possible.

One of the most common questions that I get asked is 'How often should I exercise?' Well I think that entirely depends on you as a person. But if you are a relatively sedentary person, then I would start with a couple of times a week. Once you begin to adapt over a couple of weeks, you will develop a good routine leading to healthy habits. Then you will need to increase this up to three times a week as a minimum after four weeks. Too many changes too quickly are never a good idea. It just becomes overwhelming and you will fall at the first hurdle. If I told you to increase your exercise, change your diet, cut out smoking, and eliminate alcohol by the end of the week, what would you think? Failure is inevitable. The element of change is going to take some time to get used to. You will need time to adapt to those new changes in your life. It's very hard to change and adapt if you're not used to exercising. However, you have to develop those healthy lifestyle habits somehow. My advice is that exercising 3-5 times a week will benefit your mind, body and spirit, burn excess body fat, improve posture and increasing endorphins leaving you feeling like a superstar!

Knowing how long to train for and what for is important, which is why weight training is simply a must!!

There seems to be a huge misconception that weight training is only good for 'bulking up' and increasing your size. The reality is that weight training will help you achieve all body composition goals, enabling you to become more defined and improve your posture.

Lots of women, especially, seem to think that they will turn into Arnold Schwarzenegger if they exercise with weights. It's a complete myth!! All the clients that I have trained, especially women, are consistently using a functional weights-resistance workout. Many celebrities as reported in the media use this type of workout. I guarantee they all use weight-bearing workouts. From my years of experience of working in a gym environment, the thing that makes me mad is that personal trainers these days are still using excessive cardiovascular training to try to burn those unwanted pounds despite knowing that weight training creates and stimulates muscle. Muscle is key to burning fat because it's active tissue. More muscle means an increase in metabolism resulting in an equal increase in calories burned when training or not. That combination will lead you to be lean and fit and to achieve your ideal body shape. Who doesn't want that?

Yes, there are ways to increase muscle size. But just leave those 50 kg dumbbells on the floor and see the fat melt away like butter! Your 'bingo wings' will be a thing of the past, your 'man boobs' will turn into a developed chest and your butt will look like a butt!!

Yes, my clients are often pushed to breaking point but, guess what, they value their results and they keep coming back for more!! They see incredible results and from what they have learned, they appreciate that results can only be achieved through commitment and effort. That's what it takes to get the strongest and leanest-looking body.

Listening to music while training can be a great help in maximising your motivation. Research suggests that people are more motivated when exercising if they're listening to their favourite music. One of my favourite tunes, especially when running up a hill, is the Rocky theme tune 'Eye of the Tiger'. The fact is music makes exercise more enjoyable. You will maximise your results and it's likely you will put more effort into your workout.

Another way to maximise your workout is to make sure you stick to your 'reps' (repetitions)!! We are all inclined to be a little lazy at times and if you're not being pushed, you may just 'cop out'. Laziness, boredom and lack of focus can kick in. So stick to your agreed number of reps. You will see the results if you put the reps in!

There are a number of tools out there that can help you monitor your progress. One in particular is a fantastic app called 'Coach Eye'. It shows you before and after your workout, exactly which parts of your body you need to work on and how effective your routine is in delivering results.

So it's important to find a way to be able to monitor your progress – right from the outset to the place you are going to finish. Coach Eye is a great motivating tool that shows you 'before and after' photos. By lifting heavy weights and keeping going for longer periods of time, you will start to raise your belief levels that the effort you are making is paying off. Other ways include measuring your waist size regularly and keeping track of your results in a diary or journal.

Remember by embracing change and re-energising yourself, you can use this experience as a learning journey. Explore what works for you and embrace it. Others will follow and take on board what you have learnt but, if you want to start living life, this is where it starts.

To be a great leader in the corporate world, you need to be able to manage stress effectively and ensure some relaxation time. By having a regular Swedish or sports massages, you can help reduce muscle tension, improve lymphatic drainage by reducing waste products, and help get rid of toxins in the body. Massage is a great way to relieve stress and unwanted tension. You should get a massage every fortnight or at least once a month. You really will feel the benefits, helping free tight muscles, which will improve joint mobility and posture.

One of the key problems business executives most commonly encounter is lack of time for training. One of my favourite tools for overcoming this is the 'TRX' or 'suspension trainer'. The TRX was originally designed for the US marines. However, it has proven very popular in today's fitness training environment. It can provide you with an explosive workout as it uses a range of body weight resistance, allowing pushing and pulling movement patterns that are designed to challenge the body anywhere. It's light and durable, which means it can be easily transported so it will fit in your suitcase if you're travelling a lot. It's relatively inexpensive at around £200. You can use the TRX indoors and outdoors. You can use a tree or a climbing frame to wrap it round and use as an anchor point. If indoors, you can attach it to a beam or a door.

These are my top 5 TRX exercises that will burn fat fast!

1.   Burpees:

Starting position: Body is in a prone position, feet are together and placed into the ankle straps of the TRX, hands are positioned shoulder width apart, head in alignment.

Action: Keeping the feet together, drive both knees up to the chest.

According to Oxford Dictionaries Online, the exercise was named in the 1930s after American physiologist Royal H. Burpee, who developed the Burpee test. He earned a PhD in applied physiology from Columbia University in 1940 and created the "burpee" exercise as part of his PhD thesis as a quick and simple way to assess fitness. The exercise was popularised when the United States Armed Services adopted it as a way to assess the fitness level of recruits when the US entered WWII. Consisting of a series of the exercises performed in rapid succession, the test was meant to be a quick measure of agility, coordination and strength.

2. Squats:

Starting position: Feet hip width apart, back straight, holding the TRX with hands with elbows extended, keep TRX tort, eyes looking straight ahead.

Action: Bend both knees beyond 90 degrees, buttocks as low as possible, feet flat on the ground, back straight .

3. ## Jackknife and press up combinations:

Starting position: Body is in a prone position, feet are together and placed into the ankle straps of the TRX, hands are positioned shoulder width apart, head in alignment with the spine.

Action: Keeping the feet together, drive both knees up to the chest and extend legs then lower the chest to the ground, keeping the body aligned throughout the exercise.

Perseverance is the hard work you do after you get tired of doing the hard work you already did.

Newt Gingrich

4. Hamstring curls:

Starting position: Laying on your back, feet placed through the ankle straps of the TRX, knees soft, buttocks slightly lifted.

Action: Head and shoulders stay flat on the floor, feet together, bring feet towards your buttocks whilst keeping your hips lifted.

5. Chest flys:

Starting position: Angle the body forwards approx 20-30 degrees, grip TRX with hands and straps are tort, hands positioned at chest level, head up, elbows soft.

Action: Extend the arms open whilst keeping the elbows soft.

The TRX is a great way to improve your movement patterns on your travels around the globe!

I'm going to let you in on a secret that will keep you out the gym and it goes like this... Keep your workouts short and intense.

Just like you, I too find that time is short. Even though I'm in my thirties, I feel like I'm still 21. I put being in great shape down to my short, quick and effective workouts of 30-45 minutes - absolute maximum. Get in and out as quickly as possible. How does that sound?

Seven tips to staying healthy in the office

Use these tips to help you make positive changes to your lifestyle. They all require minimum effort!

1. Replace your desk chair with a Swiss ball. This will improve your posture preventing you from slouching and placing unwanted pressure on your lower back.

2. Always have a healthy snack, e.g. a bag of nuts in your desk drawer. This will help sustain your energy levels throughout the day.

3. Keep a bottle of filtered water on your desk and drink the entire bottle (ideally glass, not plastic). Water will keep you hydrated and energised throughout the day.

4. Stay away from the coffee machine! The caffeine may initially wake you up, but shortly after you will come crashing down and you will be left feeling exhausted.

5. Get outside during your lunch hour for at least 20 minutes. All that air conditioning can have an effect on your skin, eyes and energy levels, so go out and get some good old-fashioned fresh air!

6. Improve your workstation ergonomics by just taking a few moments to assess the position of your desk, chair, keyboard and computer screen. All these factors have a direct impact on your comfort and posture.

7. Take the stairs, not the lift - unless it's on the 25th floor and above.

In order to increase your exercise adherence, find a sport or health routine that you love. It can also help to have an exercise buddy. You can push each other to succeed and you will probably also develop some competitive spirit to push you even a little bit further.

Tell everyone including friends, family and work peers, about your goals. People love stories, especially if you keep them informed and let them participate in your journey. If you want it might be useful to join a club or form a group with like-minded individuals. My running club, for example, helps me get focused and my coach pushes me and makes it competitive. There's also a great social dimension through building friendships and rapport.

If you are going to make the commitment to change your life, then don't do it half-heartedly. It's exactly the same scenario as being at work. If you set yourself a task or know that you have to produce a flawless performance in front of your boss or the chairman or the managing director, then you are going to pull out the stops and put in 110% effort, aren't you?

I believe that by putting in 110% effort into changing your lifestyle, you will feel the most fantastic sense of achievement, having accomplished what you set out to do. People around you will also begin to fully appreciate how serious you are. By committing 110%, people who come into contact with you will sense and see that change in you and the beneficial impact it is having on your life.

*Your diet is
a bank account.
Good food choices
are good investments.*

Bethenny Frankel

Chapter 8: Re-energising with the correct fuel

Changing your nutrition is going to have the most profound effects on your body and your health for life. Drinking alcohol excessively and overeating foods that contain unhealthy fats and sugars not only lead to developing the 'tyre' around your waistline, but also increase the amount of visceral fat around your organs. I cannot state how important it is to re-energise your life and change your body shape. Taking care of what you eat has a huge impact.

In this chapter, in particular, I am going to give you some key points about nutrition. Most of these points only require you to make small changes but the aim is that they become lifelong changes and you adopt permanent healthy habits. Initially, before any physical training programme takes place, I aim to kick-start clients' energy levels and metabolism using detoxification. This starts to improve health and, as a side effect, fat loss can be achieved.

It is imperative to understand that in order to achieve good nutrition, there are other things you need to change to sustain and achieve results. This book is designed to share the work I do with my clients. It is focused on encouraging you to make key changes to support your health and well-being so that you can live comfortably live with your body.

Oxidative stress

I have spoken very much about how stress can affect your life in many ways and the impact it can have on you and others around you. One of my biggest passions is talking about internal stress or 'oxidative' stress. Your body is made up of trillions of cells and, every second, at least a million cells goes through some sort of change. The best way to describe a cell is to understand its structure, how to keep it healthy, and the importance of healthy cells as building blocks of life.

A cell is a bit like an apple when you slice it in half. What does it start to do? That's right, it start to turn brown and begins to slowly degrade. Oxygen molecules attack the apple, hence the colour change (oxidative damage). Now, it's not just the air that we breathe that can damage our cells, but also things such as exercise, a lack of vitamins and minerals in our diet, smoking, alcohol, the environment we live in and an overexposure to sunlight, that can all have a significant effect as well. None of us can get away from all this oxidative damage. It's simply impossible, but it's not unmanageable. When oxidative damage attacks human cells, we call this free radical damage. This causes the cell to become unstable, which also causes other cells to become unstable too.

Research has suggested too much free radical damage may result in cancerous cells. Did you know that every time you take a puff of a cigarette, the smoke contains at least one billion free radicals, causing damage to cells as well as exposing them to other toxic chemical substances contained in the cigarette? Smoking not only damages cells, but also accelerates the aging process by at least 10 years.

Let me give you another example that is related to what you eat. How do you feel when you have a takeaway burger? You may often feel strangely unsatisfied, leading you to crave more food. In addition, you will probably begin to feel sluggish and tired within a short space of time. This is free radical damage.

Our bodies can repair cells over time but they must be able to cope with the workload. So it is possible to be healthy. However, we have to take responsibility for minimising the oxidative stress on the body. One of the ways of achieving this is to eat healthy foods that are natural antioxidants. Most people know that antioxidants are good for them but generally don't know why. Have you ever seen advertisements for food products that contain high levels of antioxidants or have you ever picked something up in the supermarket labelled 'contains added antioxidants'?

The best way to describe antioxidants is to imagine the sliced apple previously referred to. How can we reduce and slow that process of oxidative damage? An excellent antioxidant is lemon juice. By squeezing the juice over the apple, it forms an invisible protective barrier that slows down the degrading process. When it comes to making a change, nutrition plays a very important role but we have to understand that this begins by understanding the importance of maintaining healthy cells. Healthy cells = healthy body.

Some other foods rich in antioxidant include most fruits and vegetable, such as strawberries, blackberries, blueberries, lemons, oranges, garlic and tomatoes. Seafood, dark chocolate and red wine are further examples but there are a whole lot more. Adapting your diet so it contains high levels of antioxidants will help give you the ability to deal with stress on a more manageable scale.

Detoxification

The best way to describe detoxification is that it's similar to getting your car serviced. Every year or every 20,000 miles, your car will require a service. Included, as part of that service, is an oil change. By having your car serviced regularly, you can reliably expect to reduce your maintenance bills and that the car will last longer.

It's exactly the same with your body. If you don't get it regularly serviced and the oil changed, it will become less efficient and productive. Detoxification is great if you are feeling sluggish, have carbohydrate and sugar cravings, or have a poor metabolism, irregular bowel movements and poor energy levels. Detoxification is a great tool for help correcting most digestive issues including a leaky gut, food intolerances, irritable bowel syndrome and constipation.

It's essential to commit to your detox systems. Being in a job where you're sitting down most of the time and suffering lack of movement can often lead to fluid retention especially around the ankles, stomach and thighs. If you're a typical rail commuter, then you will probably have long days, getting up early without any time or desire for breakfast before you leave home. Coffee, grabbed on the way to work, will probably be your best friend. You may also feel short tempered, edgy and not in control of your emotions.

An increase in body fat, especially around your stomach, is also a clear indicator that you need to detox!! Otherwise the tyre around your mid-section is only going to get bigger.

Successful detoxification can also help to reverse insulin resistance as it can help remove the body's waste products and help balance blood sugar (glucose) levels.

Story: Three weeks before I completed a dissertation, I decided to do a five-day detoxification programme. I felt it was the right time and I needed a quick solution to revitalise my energy levels. I was under a huge amount of stress. I had assignment deadlines to meet, other coursework due as well as business and family commitments. I felt quite overwhelmed! My detox included low-glycaemic nutritional smoothies and shakes, low-glycaemic nutritional snack bars, potent multivitamins and omega-3 fish oils. After a week, I felt absolutely amazing, re-energised, focused, and calm. The detox gave me the means to deal with my stress levels effectively. My friends and family made various comments, such as 'You look different, fresh and invigorated'.

Your liver is the third most important organ in your body. It is where the detox process needs to take place, as the liver is responsible for metabolising the food we consume into the nutrients the body needs for energy and a healthy system. There are certain things that can interfere with liver function. These include alcohol, pesticides, oestrogen (high levels of oestrogen in men can lead to the growth of breast tissue: 'moobs' or 'man boobs'), medication, refined sugar, and trans-fatty acids.

A common question that I often get asked is how often should I detox? Well, a detox doesn't necessarily need to be for very long. It can range from just 5 days, although some people up choose programmes that continue for months on end.

I would recommend that you detox at least every six months. This will help you develop a routine of healthy eating, balance your blood sugar levels, create healthy eating habits and correct digestive issues. Detoxing will give you the kick-start your body so desperately needs.

Here are some very simple steps for you to take to help with this process.

Phase 1:

Increase B vitamins: these types of foods contain powerful antioxidants. They are also known as energy foods and include foods such as oysters, mussels, liver, caviar, mackerel, lean beef, lamb, Swiss cheeses (in moderation) and duck eggs (chicken eggs are OK too but have less vitamin B12 in them).

Phase 2:

Increase the sulphur in your diet (supplementation is not required): these types of foods increase immune system function, support liver function, and have anti-cancer properties.

They also contain amino acids (the building blocks to cell regeneration and recovery). They include foods such as beef, chicken, egg yolks, onions, shallots, leeks and garlic.

Use this checklist to help with your digestion

1. Eat slowly and chew your food: it enables the stomach to more readily break food down.

2. Drink water in between meals

3. Eat 'real' food, i.e. fresh food that you prepare yourself, not microwave ready meals.

4. Include probiotics in your diet: probiotics contain friendly bacteria for your gut for its health and harmony. Probiotics can be found in yogurt mainly.

5. Be regular: a well-functioning digestion system will help you become more regular. If you don't have a regular cycle, this can lead to the body holding onto unnecessary waste products and toxins.

6. Stimulate your digestion by drinking hot water with a slice of lemon on a daily basis.

7. Include a variety of berries, such as blueberries, strawberries, blackcurrants, redcurrants and blackberries, in your diet.

The Glycaemic Index

The world of nutrition is a confusing place for many people. There are so many mixed messages about what to eat or what not to eat. It's no wonder we're left scratching our heads. I remember when I was at school; we were taught about the conventional 'food pyramid', which was originally designed to fight the surge in heart disease in the 1960s. The food pyramid helped give the population nutritional advice on what foods to eat on a daily basis. This clearly isn't working for us anymore, as our lifestyles are very different from that of over 50 years ago.

One of the causes of the high levels of obesity we are seeing in Western society could be down to the fact that I still hear talk of the need to eat six to eleven servings of bread, potatoes, cereal, and rice daily, together with five portions of fruits and vegetables and two to three servings of meat, poultry, nuts, milk, yogurt, cheeses daily, and fats and oils used sparingly.

This is a myth and clearly has failed society and left our nations with a major health epidemic, not to forget to mention that people are exercising less and job habits have changed. I'm going to show you my very own food pyramid that I think everyone should use. It really does work! It's called the 40:30:30 diet. That means your diet should consist of 40% carbohydrate, 30% protein and 30% healthy fats.

I especially advocate using the glycaemic index as it really works. The glycaemic index is used to estimate how much each particular carbohydrate in a food raises blood glucose levels relative to pure glucose, and how quickly your blood sugar levels will rise after eating a particular food. Foods are placed in a table called the glycaemic index (GI). The higher the GI, the faster the glucose gets released into the blood stream. Glucose has a GI of 100 whereas an apple has a GI of around 24. What I really love about the glycaemic index is that it is related to how much energy you get from a particular food and over what period of time.

What is your general routine at lunch? What do you buy most often? Do you tend to buy a sandwich, panini, and sausage roll? Now how do you feel immediately after your lunch, and how do you feel 45 minutes later?

Write down your thoughts

Understanding your reaction to food is very important as it generally makes you aware of how it makes you feel, whether you feel energetic or not, bloated or not, or if you feel satisfied or not. By understanding your reactions, you can then make sound decisions of what foods to consume. From my past experience, when I eat pasta, for example, I generally feel sluggish and I want to fall asleep. Do you ever get a similar feeling when you eat a particular food? One of the key steps you need to take in monitoring what you eat to is to keep a food diary. I find the best way to keep a food dairy is to keep track of two days out of the working week and one day from the weekend as your eating habits are likely to be different.

Write out your food diary so that you understand it. Include a description of how you feel after immediately consuming a particular food and then 30 minutes later. The point to recording what you consume is to create awareness and to get it to act as a 'wake-up call'. You need to take accountability and if you're going to change, you need to know what to eat and how you're going to change your diet.

Many people will relate to the following scenario: at about 2-3pm, you experience a general dip in energy. This general feeling of 'slowing down' starts to spread amongst your colleagues throughout the office. One makes a passing comment and says, "I'm hungry". As energy levels start to dwindle, one person goes to the vending machine to purchase a milk chocolate bar and a coffee, then somebody else does, then another and another and so forth. Everyone is suddenly buzzing around. People are lively and start 'bouncing off the walls'! Have you ever experienced something like that in your work environment? Then suddenly, 20-30 minutes later, the novelty has worn off, energy levels dip again and it's all gone quiet. People become less productive and start staring at the clock, counting down the minutes. This is what I called the 'glycaemic crash'.

Let me give you another example. One of the UK's favourite foods is mashed potato. Now a potato is grown in soil, which has generally been over-farmed. Then you peel the potato (the most nutritious part is the skin). You then tend to over-boil it until it crumbles, and then mash it up. Most of the nutrients are therefore lost through the cooking process. The potato is a food with one of the highest scores on the glycaemic index - 94 compared to table sugar that has a glycaemic score of 74. An alternative to potato is sweet potato that has an average glycaemic rating of just 19.

When you consume something that is generally high in glycaemic such as a milk chocolate bar, white rice, pasta, your blood sugar levels will rise. This then sends a message to the brain, and then to the pancreas to release insulin in order to return blood sugar levels to normal. However, when the pancreas releases insulin, it doesn't know how much to release and can often release too much insulin as a consequence. I call this the overspill. As a result of the overspill, blood sugar levels drop rapidly below normal blood sugar levels. This then triggers hunger and 'carb' cravings kick in.

You will most likely make a decision either to eat something else that will satisfy your hunger or alternatively be disciplined and not eat at all, forcing the body to release two hormones, adrenalin and cortisol (stress hormones) to balance your blood sugar levels. If you had decided to eat something carb-based, then this forms a 'rollercoaster' effect where you get 'highs' and 'lows' throughout the day, leaving the pancreas overworked and exhausted. If this is you, then be aware that one day your pancreas will give up on you. That's a fact and you may become diabetic for life.

Many people working in offices may tend to be overweight and the main reason for this is insulin, which is what I call the fat hormone!! So insulin makes you fat. But also one other factor is stress. Stress can keep your blood sugar level elevated due to high levels of cortisol and adrenalin.

The key point I'm trying to make is that, if you want a more sustained source of energy, then choose low glycaemic foods, moderate to medium, and avoid high glycaemic foods all together. If you are conscious of your weight, don't be too concerned about your fat consumption, but check your sugar consumption. The UK government guideline daily is 100g.

When clients come to me asking for my help, I always ask them if they are going to embrace the changes I suggest for them. As part of this, I will always ask them to create a food diary at the beginning of my 12-week programme. With your typically high-pressured and stressed lifestyle, it's vital that you acknowledge that your mind, body and nutrition come first!! I always ask clients to write out their food diary for two days during the normal working week and for one day from the weekend. This, in most cases, is a big wake-up call. I believe that 70% of the health improvements you need to make can simply be achieved by changing your nutritional habits. With your food diary, you can see where you are going wrong and then can start to make improvements.

If you're going to follow my advice about the glycaemic index and sustain energy over a long time period, you are going to need to 'refuel' every 2-3 hours. Your metabolism is key to burning fat the natural way. If you have a high metabolism, then it will be easier for you to burn calories when you are not exercising at all. Who doesn't want that? If you go for long periods of time without eating, the body will need to find an additional energy source to feed off, which is muscle. Muscle helps because it is active tissue. The more muscle we have, the leaner we will look. So don't let your metabolism drop: that's key or your body will start to eat itself and you will hold onto your excess fat.

There is an important window of opportunity to fire up your metabolism and this is normally first thing in the morning. After sleeping for a long period of time without food, your body will be craving for its 'fuel'. Fire up your metabolism and keep the fire alive by regularly re-fuelling throughout the day! This will turn your body from a sluggish fat storage warehouse into a natural fat burning machine. If you want to achieve the body of your dreams, my advice is to never go hungry!

One of the other things that you need to consider very seriously is alcohol intake, even after a detoxification process. Alcohol is not only calorific but it will prevent you from burning fat. It also interferes with the function of the liver. Throughout my 12-week programme, I tell my clients that, although it's not forever, if they are serious about the programme and change, then no alcohol. Experience has shown me that clients' body shape and lifestyle will only improve if alcohol is removed from the equation.

As part of the detoxification process, I have a list of rules throughout the programme and one of these is cutting down on caffeine. You are probably stressed enough and by drinking caffeine, you are simply making your symptoms worse.

Story: A friend of mine is really into martial arts. However, his job as a sales executive comes with huge responsibilities and stress. He lives off Red Bull. He probably drinks at least 5 or 6 cans a day. This increases that nasty hormone cortisol that I was talking about. He believes that drinking Red Bull keeps him alert. Well, actually, I would say he is becoming a sugar addict. The stimulants and the huge sugar content of energy drinks can get you hooked in the same way that a heroin addict needs a constant fix. Increased cortisol = increase fat levels and an overworked pancreas. Insulin makes you FAT!!

If you're a regular coffee drinker and think drinking decaffeinated coffee is a better option, then unfortunately that's not the case. Caffeinated coffee generally contains toxic chemicals. My advice is to swap your coffee or energy drink for a green tea, or red bush and peppermint tea, or stick to water!! In the evening, chamomile tea is very good for distressing as well. Cutting out caffeine may seem quite hard initially, but it is well worth it and you will benefit both mentally and physically.

Eat lots and lots of dark, green leafy vegetables. Not only are they nutritious but they're also full of antioxidants. Green leafy vegetables include spinach, asparagus, savoy cabbage, curly kale and broccoli. The best way to eat them is raw. Nutrients can be lost through the cooking process.

One of the questions I get asked most about is supplements!! Some people and even health professionals say that you simply don't need to take supplements. You can get all your nutrients from your food. Well that simply is not the case anymore. Times change. An orange these days contain less nutrients then it did 30 years ago. An increase in the use of pesticides and fertilisers, over farming, plus reliance on greater amounts of imported fruits and vegetables especially in the UK means our food loses vital nutrients. We should all take supplements even if we eat a totally organic diet.

Supplements are there to complement a healthy diet, not replace it!! I always carry out an initial lifestyle appraisal for my clients and, in all cases, they are lacking essential vitamins and minerals.

The first supplement that I recommend taking is omega-3 fish oils, not cod liver oil, which some people think is the same. Additional, omega-3 in your diet will supply you with an additional energy source from the 'healthy fats' it contains. Omega-3 also aids brain function and helps reduce inflammation (especially that caused by exercise), and increases focus and concentration levels. However, the biggest benefit is that it helps fight stress. Everyone that I have trained has seen positive changes within the first two weeks of the programme. Omega-3 is also contained in oily fish, such as mackerel, sardines and kippers. However, you need to consume a minimum of three servings of oily fish weekly to benefit fully.

For general health, I consider multivitamins 'a must', especially those that include a wide range of vitamins and minerals. However, you should be very cautious about which multivitamins you purchase. There are some key questions you need to ask yourself. Are they potent? Are they third party-tested? Have they been tested for purity? Do they meet pharmaceutical standards? Read carefully what each multivitamin tablet contains and how it is manufactured, etc. Three out of four supplements are contaminated and may contain harmful and banned substances, such as lead and mercury. So do your research (Fox, M. 2010).

Check out this website - xclusivenutrition.usana.com - and fill in the free health assessment online. It will provide a personalised and customised assessment of your various nutritional requirements. The products they manufacture are free of contaminants but also made to the same standards as our drug laws that are far much stringent than food laws.

Eat only until you feel satisfied!! That's not the same as feeling like a stuffed pig! In certain situations, especially if you have been invited to a meal, many people feel obligated to eat everything on the plate. Don't feel like that!! Eating too much is a main reason why people are becoming fatter. In Western countries, especially in places like the United States, portions sizes are humongous. Many of us no longer know when to stop eating, with food often becoming an addiction. Your body can only absorb a certain amount of nutrients from foods at a time, the rest is stored as excess body fat. Typically, people with busy working lives often develop the habit of consuming large amounts of food in one 'hit', normally as a large evening meal. However, your energy levels and metabolism cannot be sustained through this method.

When thinking about the food you buy, think 'organic'! Although organic foods may cost a little extra, they are still excellent value as they can contain up to five times more nutrients and antioxidants. If, like me, you have a love for super cars, think of the most beautiful and elegant Ferrari or Lamborghini you have seen: it's shiny and glossy and the engine roars. When you fill the tank up, you're not going to fill it up with the poor quality fuel, you're going to fill it with the best! It's exactly the same with your body. The best fuel will work to sustain your body operating at the optimum level. Look after your body and it will look after you.

Some organic foods can sometimes be very hard to get hold at certain times of the year. However, there are two essential organic foods - eggs (ideally omega-3) and chicken - which are normally always readily available. If however, organic produce is unavailable, always go for the next best thing, which is free-range.

Have you ever heard the saying, 'Breakfast is the most important meal of the day'? Well, it's true. Ensure you eat breakfast and set yourself up for your day! Avoid the temptation of relying on a series of frequent caffeine hits from your local Starbucks to get you through a busy morning.

'Crash and burn' is all that will happen. The best breakfasts are protein-based, and my favourite is eggs. Protein will keep you fuller for longer, sustain your energy levels for longer and satisfy your appetite. Egg doesn't take a huge amount of time to cook. Have them scrambled, poached or boiled, but without bread!! If you still love your porridge, then that's no problem. Just make sure you add nuts and seeds.

I don't expect you to be good 100% of the time, but I do expect you to be consistent eight out of ten times - after all, we are only human. If you try too hard to be 100% perfect with your diet all the time, you will fail and no one likes to fail. So get some balance and give yourself some room.

Have a 'cheat day' occasionally because you deserve it. If you achieve a goal, your reward to yourself could be to eat that big cream cake or a chocolate bar. We are still human after all and I don't think it's unreasonable to have a treat so don't feel guilty or negative if you eat something regarded as a treat. But we must still be accountable and responsible for what we eat. As you know, eating too much of the wrong type of food is bad for body and mind. Allowing yourself an occasional 'cheat day' lets you to look forward to having those 'treat' foods without feeling guilty about them. There is no need to be too extreme; it will only screw up your results!

Which brings me to my next subject - especially designed for weight conscious executives!! Yes, if you know that you need to lose weight, you're right that you need to cut down on the amount of food you're putting into your body. If you take my advice on board, then you will not only become healthier, but you will lose weight naturally. My advice is not to become addicted to the scales. When you weigh yourself, the scales don't take your muscle and water content into consideration. Measure your energy levels and waist size, if you want to measure your progress.

One of the questions my clients most frequently ask me is 'What if I have to work during my lunch hour?' I really do understand that when you're busy at work - running a team, networking with potential clients, securing deals or meeting deadlines, etc. – then lunchtime eating can often be forgotten. But your health is just as important as your work – probably more so!! So if you're saying lunch is 'impossible', think about what you are saying. If you commit to making time for a healthy lunchtime snack with the same passion and dedication you give to your work and career, then I believe you can make it happen. Improving your lifestyle is not only going to benefit you in the long term but also offset some of your unwanted stress, especially from alcohol and rich restaurant foods.

So let me help you... Eat a handful of nuts and lean meats before heading out.

1. Avoid buffet style or 'eat all you can' restaurants

2. Don't go out on an empty stomach

3. Go for the salad bar minus the fatty dressings. Note that balsamic vinegar, French dressing and olive oil are fine)

4. Stay away from the dreaded bread basket!!

5. Go for items on the menu that have been prepared healthily, such as boiled, steamed and roasted vegetables

6. Keep low GI in mind and order the most suitable choice available

7. Limit your intake of alcohol beverages

10 nutrition challenges

1. Never skip breakfast

2. Eat three main meals and two snacks daily

3. Drink a 1.5 litre bottle of water daily. Your body is made of around 70% water so it's obvious how important keeping hydrated is for survival. Poor concentration levels and poor training can lead you to feeling tired and thirsty. If you are thirsty as you read this book, you are already dehydrated! Drink water regularly throughout the day

4. Eat protein with every meal

5. Stay away from bread, potatoes and pasta

6. Avoid breakfast cereal. Most breakfast cereals contain more sugar than a can of Coke. I call cereal the 'devil's food'!!

7. Avoid fried fatty foods as most are cooked in trans-fatty acids. Most of these foods have a high calorie content and low nutrient content

8. Stay away from the microwave. Microwave meals generally consist of highly processed 'fake' food which contains excess amounts of sodium, increasing your blood pressure and increasing your risks of coronary heart disease

9. Cook 'fresh' at every occasion. Preparing food is a learning experience. It will also take you on an educational journey to learn what's good for you and what foods make you healthy

10. Avoid fruit juices. Many people think that fruit juices are healthy and contribute towards our 'five-a-day'. But they're wrong. Most juices, especially those from concentrate, contain more sugar than a can of fizzy drink. Excess sugar in your diet means excess fat

5 nutrition challenges whilst abroad

1.   Find out in advance the foods that the hotel typically serves

2.   Locate the nearest grocery store that serve a range of organic, whole and fresh produce (whole foods is generally a good choice)

3.   Use only bottled water or filtered water; it is much healthier (most tap water is generally unsafe and untreated, it generally has high amounts of fluoride. Fluoride is a toxic substance that is linked to a range of health concerns such as bone diseases, brain effects, skeletal fluorosis, endocrine disruption and fertility problems)

4.   Locate markets with fresh produce

5.   Check cooked or fresh food before consuming it: different countries have different hygiene and food standards. If it doesn't look good or it's lukewarm in temperature, don't touch it and ask for a fresh dish

Here are some quick nutritious meals that take 10-15 minutes to prepare. So you can easily incorporate them into your routine:

1. Vegetable omelette – 2or 3 eggs (organic or free-range) with chopped vegetables of your own choice.

2. Grilled haddock with mixed vegetables and sweet potatoes

3. Tuna jacket sweet potato - bake a sweet potato and fill with fresh or tinned tuna, low fat mayo, sweetcorn and steamed broccoli

4. Baked salmon with almonds, served with asparagus, broccoli, sweetcorn and sweet potato

5. Shish kebab - place lean steak, turkey or chicken on a skewer with peppers, onions, mushrooms. Then grill. Serve with vegetables

6. 'Chef's salad': lean turkey, ham or chicken with a sliced hard-boiled egg, teaspoon of low fat cheese, mixed vegetables, lettuce, tomatoes, guacamole and fat-free dressing

Chapter 9: Invest in yourself

Celebrate! Yes, you have achieved it; you have fulfilled your destiny. If you have completed the tasks and activities in the book, then your journey is coming to an end… but not quite yet.

Before I show you how to invest in yourself, you need to know why investment in yourself is important.

Your journey through this book should have given you valuable lessons and one of those lessons is to begin to value your life and those around you. Be thankful for your support networks, friends, work colleagues and family members and even me! You also should now have a refocused purpose in life: able to view your life now compared to what it was before. Your goal in life is not just about work, work, work, it's about establishing a work/life balance by achieving a positive mindset using fitness, nutritional and lifestyle strategies that work for you.

On that note, it's important to invest not just in yourself but also in your family!! You will find that the lifestyle you create will have an impact on your family in particular. Your life will be fulfilled when you are able to attend your son or daughter's sports day, pick them up from school every now and then, and have a family dinner together. If you want to get more out of your life, then it's important to think of others before yourself.

By working long, ridiculous hours, you're not doing it for them, you're doing it for yourself!! The only person that puts unnecessary stress into your life is you! With the clients that I've worked with, I've found that, in 95% of cases, arguments with their loved ones are the result of long hours at work. If you believe you need to work more hours to get away from arguments and nagging, it's because of your own insecurity.

You're simply satisfying your ego. Your priority should be to put your family first. We all have choices in life. Whether you make the right choice and love your life is down to you!

As a decision-maker, you have the power to share your positive experiences to create a vibrant work culture. Your team will begin to evolve and send out the clear message that 'If you want more out of life, then live it'. Your team will become more productive. They will be more creative thinkers and more motivated. And it will all be because of you. Your positive vibrant work ethic will not just make your team happy, but will also allow them to deliver better results while reducing unnecessary pressures.

As people around you start to notice the positive change in you, recognition will start to fly in from everywhere. You'll get comments such as 'Congratulations! You have done a fantastic job'. As you become more motivated, your enthusiasm increases; you smile more and generally look more relaxed and happy. You're able to close more business deals because 'your enthusiasm speaks a thousand words'.

Let's quickly backtrack to where I talked about 'the self'. I want you to go back to when you started on this journey. I spoke about your 'present self' and your 'ideal self'. What was that image that you had locked up in your mind? What were the characteristics, personality, and attitudes you attributed to your ideal self? Now the big question is do you feel like you're now more aligned to your ideal self? Or does it feel like you've still got a long way to go? If the answer is you still feel miles away, then did you complete the tasks fully as set out for you and have you been honest with yourself? Go back if you haven't completed the activities set out and dedicate some time for yourself. If you have completed the tasks, and you and others do see the change, then great! I congratulate you!

Staying aligned with your ideal self is very important because it means you're able to stay on track and keep motivated. You can do this by reviewing your goals and setting new challenges. In order to stay motivated, you should look for innovative and creative ways to keep yourself interested. As you adapt, you must consistently look for the next big thing, whatever it may be.

To start investing in yourself, I recommend making a list of hobbies and interests that you would like to do more of and put a date in your diary of when you are going to start doing them. It could be playing with model trains, going out cycling, fishing, salsa classes, cooking or playing cricket, etc. but make sure you spend time doing it at least three times a week. I would also recommend you make up a 'bucket' list of all the things you want to do. It could be to train as a scuba diver, it could be to write a book, or see the Seven Wonders of the World, etc. Whatever it may be, get it in that bucket! The next thing to do is to prioritise what you're going to do first and when you're going to do it. Some things in your bucket list might not happen for ten years, but it will definitely give you something to look forward to!

My 12-week programmes aren't for the faint-hearted but if you do ultimately achieve your goals, you will begin to see changes not just in your mind but also in your body. Most of my clients normally need to get a new wardrobe because they have dropped a dress or waist size, so I often advise them to get a personal shopper. You're going to look amazing when you look in the mirror. You will see a new you and you will have 'sex appeal'!

"Purpose is what gives life a meaning."

C H Parkhurst

My life is fulfilled

In order to fulfil the promise to yourself of making change, you simple need to stay in that positive mindset and consistently work on yourself.

As I mentioned before with regards to Adam's hierarchy of human needs, let me ask you a question: are you on the road to achieving self-actualisation? Most people don't ever achieve self-actualisation, purely because they don't believe in themselves. However, you should work your hardest to push towards that goal. Nelson Mandela is known for tackling apartheid, poverty and inequality in South Africa. Mother Teresa is known for setting up hospices and homes for people with HIV/Aids, orphanages and providing help for poorest of the poor. These are extreme cases, but you too can make an impact by helping others.

One of the ways on how I get my clients to focus is to visualise. This is a very powerful tool. Close your eyes and create a thought in your head. What do you see? Do you see yourself getting on stage and being recognised as Manager of the Year? Do you see yourself sprinting across the finish line in a marathon, or it could be seeing yourself on that sandy beach in Barbados. Powerful, isn't it? How does it make you feel? What do you need to do? I recommend you visualise at least twice a day for at least 10 minutes each time. Use this time to really feel, touch and become part of that experience.

Get yourself booked into Bikram yoga. Bikram yoga is series of yoga postures and breathing techniques performed in a heated room. The yoga posture sequences will help maximise oxygenation and detoxification of the entire body. It is a fantastic way to develop strength and flexibility and to counter a sedentary lifestyle. It brings with it body vitality, health and a sense of complete well-being. The heat will help facilitate stretching and prevention of injuries and promote sweating which is very useful in helping the body remove waste products.

You can also develop positive thinking by simply changing your environment more often. Changing your environment is stimulating to the body and mind. The change could be a walk in the country, enjoying the sights of the beach or listening to calming music, which can be very helpful in winding down after a busy day.

By being more positive, you are simply building your self-confidence, and there are a number of ways to do this. One approach is to go out and do more networking and strengthen relationships with friends. Another is to go out socialising with a group of friends or a partner to a bar; this will help promote a positive mindset. Thirdly, take regular breaks. These will allow you to reflect on how your day has gone, what you have achieved and ways to do things better.

One of the biggest things that truly relaxes me is sitting on a sandy beach, closing my eyes and listening to the waves of the sea. Meditation is proven to help the mind rest and relax. The energy from your imagined waves will give you a sense of peace and tranquilly. Do this for 15-20 minutes every other day.

There are many different ways to meditate and I would recommend you explore which one works for you. The simplest way is to simply stop what you are doing right now!! Just take a second and breathe, switch off and empty all your thoughts. The only thing that you need to concentrate on is inhaling and exhaling. What do you feel? Relief, calmness, or nothing??

You don't need to be locked away from civilisation to enjoy meditation. Enjoy the moment you are living in: don't be weighed down by other people or your schedule. Just taking that moment in your life will give you abundance in return. Regular practice of 'being in that moment' will enable you to experience a greater sense of clarity, balance, positivity and energy that you can take with you for the rest of your day and your life.

You can't put a limit on anything. The more you dream, the farther you get.

Michael Phelps

Now it's all about maintenance and keeping up your hard work.

Tip: Keep a journal and write it up daily. Write down what you have done today, what challenges you have encountered, how you overcame them and what your achievements were.

Set yourself weekly goals that maintain your focus and drive. Inspirational leaders are not born, they are made. What is it you wish to achieve? What are your lifetime ambitions?

When setting a goal, dream 'big' and you will believe in it.

Story: Michael Phelps is one the greatest Olympians that ever lived. Phelps speaks very much about the origins of his success and how from an early age setting goals in his life became vitally important. He received this advice from his two older sisters and, from the age of seven, started to regularly set goals. At the age of 11, his coach told him if he worked hard enough, he would be good enough to compete in the next Olympics in Sydney in 2000. So he got to work and became the youngest American swimmer in 68 years to compete in the Olympics. In 2001 at the age of 15, he then went on to break the world record in the 200 metre butterfly. But that simply was not enough. In the 2004 Olympic games in Athens, he won six gold medals but wanted to push the bar even higher. Competing in the Beijing Olympics in 2008, he had already earned six gold medals, but then, with two more races to run, he began to feel tired and demotivated. He said to his coach: "I have nothing left. I'm drained." With the help of his coach and through his own determination, he managed to finish the last two races purely on sheer adrenalin, bringing his total of gold medals at Beijing to eight. In addition, he broke the world record in every event he competed in except one. His quote is: *"Dream big and never give up."*

Read personal development books. They will teach you how to grow into a bigger and better person, and help you develop your creative thinking abilities and start new beginnings.

How do you view your life? Is it fulfilled yet? If you haven't quite got there yet, don't worry. The most important thing is working on getting there. It's not a race. You're not in competition with anyone else. It's just you. Having a fulfilled life should mean happiness. How do you view happiness? What does it look like?

Happiness is personal to each of us but it does share universal characteristics. Happiness is about living in harmony. This means the more you understand and are at ease with who you are and your abilities, the more likely you are to understand and appreciate the rest of humanity. Harmony is a feeling that you are happy and content, and that your mind and emotions are well balanced. Happiness is about valuing your treasured moments with life, time with friends and family, and never taking life for granted. You never know what's around the corner! Someone who is truly fulfilled detaches themselves from the ego, recognising that by just existing, they are touching the lives of others. My recommendation is do something for other people. In the past, I have helped raise thousands of pounds for children's charities by participating in regular running events. I have also helped run and support community groups that encourage young people to participate in sports.

Do something for charity, whether that is volunteering to work on health programmes in Africa or running in the London Marathon for a cancer charity, moves you up towards that journey of self-actualisation.

Giving something back could involve you being part of a community group, such as the Scouts or Guides, a business start-up community group or a networking business event.

Having a fulfilled life means also needing and wanting success. What do you want to be successful at? What do you want to be known for? What do you want to expand your knowledge in?

You do can be successful at anything you want to be. When I mention the words 'success' or 'successful people', what comes to mind? Being successful is having the feeling of a sense of accomplishment. You have conquered and mastered your ambitions and you have found solutions that work for you. Who would you like to dedicate your success to? Some of the great success stories that come to mind reflect the skills covered in this book. It's all about believing in yourself and having commitment.

Walt Disney was fired from a newspaper because they say he lacked imagination and had no good ideas. He is an international icon and the Disney Corporation is now worth $36 billion.

When Thomas Edison was young, his teacher told him that he was too stupid to learn anything. Yet after perseverance and failing over a thousand times, he invented the light bulb.

J.K. Rowling has gone from 'rags to riches'. Her first husband left her and she had to bring up a young daughter by herself. Now as a result of the famous 'Harry Potter' novels, she is one of the most successful authors of our time.

The point I'm making is that you don't have to be a superstar to succeed. Whenever someone says, "You're not talented enough", "You're not good enough" or "You can't achieve that", simply don't accept it!! Believe in yourself and ignore such distractions. You will put yourself on track for achieving total well-being.

My 12-week programmes are designed to help successful business leaders and executives work smarter, not harder. I can empower you to make the right choices, re-energise your body, mind and spirit, and help you succeed in life. Living your life is about living it on your terms and developing a healthy work life/balance that works for you and your family.

*Success is knowing
your purpose in life,
growing to reach your
maximum potential,
and sowing seeds
that benefit others.*

John Maxwell

It's time for action

This is the end of my book and, in celebration, I'm going to see the big screening of 'Charlie and the Chocolate Factory' at the Drury Lane Theatre in London with my son. Now you can do one of two things with this book: either place it on a bookshelf to gather dust and continue with your busy stressed life; or you can use it to create a new beginning - a whole new way to live your life. How many books have you read on fitness, nutrition or health? Don't use this book just to accompany some new 'fad' diet. You will get discouraged and it will be something you will want to forget.

It's time for **implementation** and this is where the fun part starts. I want you to succeed and I'm confident you can. It's up to you. Taking control of your health should be your number one priority, especially if you want to be successful leader. Your health will reflect what happens in the workplace and the business deals that you are able to close. Whenever your life becomes uncontrollable, ask yourself **'why'**. Was it achieving more with your work career? Was it to get a good night's sleep? Maybe all you wanted was to spend some quality time with the family and have the energy to enjoy it to. Be very clear about your 'why'.

This book sets out a path. But you have to choose which path you will take. So choose the path that gives you joy in abundance. Remember to have a plan that is simple, easy-to-follow and enjoyable. Don't forget to enjoy your life. Book that holiday, attend that sports day or do something stupendous, such as when I hiked across the Grand Canyon!

Take control of your health before it's too late and see a professional to discuss your health and fitness plan. Focus on the three main aspects of well-being: psychological (mindset), nutrition (energy) and physiological (body and stress management). You will notice in a short period of time that you will begin to sleep better, have more energy, be more productive and focused.

Make lifestyle changes and celebrate them. Turn off all work communication after 7pm. Use a Swiss ball instead of a chair at your desk. Commit to getting fresh air for at least 60 minutes every day. These are big things - so don't overlook them.

By now, you should have a better understanding of how health and stress management go hand in hand, and what can go wrong if you don't do something about them. You understand that your thoughts about work/life balance can change your mindset, energy levels and motivation. You are ready to ask for expert help and, by using one of our programmes, we can help you achieve a distressed life and a re-energised body and mind. If you just have a small belief, then hold on to it and build on it.

I believe that every senior business executive can achieve a good work/life balance and feel de-stressed and inspired. You will see a transformation like none other. You'll feel and look great, and others around you will notice too. You will be oozing self-confidence and a positive ego and have a profound positive impact on others, leaving you feeling so much younger. Now that's something worth celebrating!

For those of you who want ongoing support, or to share challenges, stories, frustrations and celebrations, you can join others on our social media sites devoted to this book.

Stepping up and taking you to the next level

After reading this book, you may feel inspired to make changes to your lifestyle and learn more of how exercise, nutrition or mental well-being can impact your life positively. As with the many things in life, reading a book is one thing, but doing something from what you have learnt is another.

Adam Strong's company Xclusive Corporate Fitness regularly run group/team fitness masterclasses, seminars, discussions and health days.

Adam also offers one-day workshops for organisations on the back of the book. You can keep in touch with Adam on:

www.xclusivecorporatefitness.com/blog/

www.twitter.com/adamistrong

www.linkedin.com/in/adamistrong

*A real decision
is measured
by the fact that
you've taken a
new action.
If there's no action,
you haven't
truly decided.*

Tony Robbins

If you would like to review this book, we will reward you for taking your time for doing so. Here's how:

1. Write a review of this book

2. Post it on the following: Amazon, iTunes bookstore, your Facebook page or your blog

3. Send the link or a screenshot to the following email address: adam@xclusivecorporatefitness.com

4. One of the team will contact you or your company to arrange a free 45 minute consultation (worth £200), subject to distance you are located, or samples of new products/services from Xclusive Corporate Fitness

Bibliography

April 12 2007. *'Why Should We Get Eight Hours Sleep?* BBC News. http://news.bbc.co.uk. Accessed July 29th 2013

Back Pain (nd) available online: http://www.enetmd.com/content/back-pain. Accessed July 29th 2013

CERIELLO A and MOTZ E (2004) *Is Oxidative Stress The Pathogenic Mechanism Underlying Insulin Resistance, Diabetes And Cardiovascular Disease?* Arteriosclerosis, Thrombosis and Vascular biology. 24, 816-823

CHAPMAN L (2012) Stress in the City. *Therapy Today.* Vol 23, Issue 1

COHEN JS (2001) *Overdose: The Case Against The Drug Companies.* 1st Edition, New York, New York: Penguin Putman

FOX M (2010) *U.S Dietary Supplements Often Contaminated Report.* Availiable online: http://www.reuters.com/article/2010/08/03/us-usa-supplements-idUSTRE6721F520100803

VAN GAAL L, MERTENS I and DE BLOCK C (2006) Mechanisms Linking Obesity With Cardiovascular Disease. *Nature.* 444, 875-880

WHIPPLE T (2011) *Banks Keep Shtoom About Stress In The City.* The Times. http://www.thetimes.co.uk/tto/life/article3219288.ece